Manag₍

GOLF

What's Your Handicap?

Management

GOLF

What's Your Handicap?

Michael J. Kami • **William Martz**

S^{t}_{L}

St. Lucie Press
Boca Raton, Florida

Library of Congress Cataloging-in-Publication Data

Catalog information may be obtained from the Library of Congress

This book contains information obtained from authentic and highly regarded sources. Reprinted material is quoted with permission, and sources are indicated. A wide variety of references are listed. Reasonable efforts have been made to publish reliable data and information, but the author and the publisher cannot assume responsibility for the validity of all materials or for the consequences of their use.

Neither this book nor any part may be reproduced or transmitted in any form or by any means, electronic or mechanical, including photocopying, microfilming, and recording, or by any information storage or retrieval system, without prior permission in writing from the publisher.

The consent of CRC Press LLC does not extend to copying for general distribution, for promotion, for creating new works, or for resale. Specific permission must be obtained in writing from CRC Press LLC for such copying.

Direct all inquiries to CRC Press LLC, 2000 Corporate Blvd., N.W., Boca Raton, Florida 33431.

© 1998 by CRC Press LLC
St. Lucie Press is an imprint of CRC Press LLC

No claim to original U.S. Government works
International Standard Book Number 1-57444-105-1
Printed in the United States of America 1 2 3 4 5 6 7 8 9 0
Printed on acid-free paper

CONTENTS

This book is dedicated to Kay Kami and Lou Martz,
two wonderful wives whose patience and tolerance have no par.

Management is a lot like golf. You must choose correctly from a
variety of clubs to make the right shot. It does not help much to
birdie one hole if you double bogey the next two. You've got to do
pretty well on all eighteen holes. Then, there's the rough, the hazards and going out of bounds. Discouraging? Not at all...You can
always improve your game.

William Vaughn, ex-Eastman Kodak
(Mr. Vaughn did not follow his own advice
in his later years at Kodak,
but his original statement fits very well
with the key concept of this book)

PREFACE

The authors have been good friends for many years. They co-authored in 1979 the *Strategic Planning Manual*, which became a working tool for many companies, large and small. It was translated into several languages and used throughout the world. Both authors are top-management consultants with practical experience in diverse industries. They strongly believe in action-oriented planning, resulting in speedy execution and good things actually happening. They cringe at neatly bound reams of paper, full of promises but generating no constructive activity.

The purpose of this book is to stimulate a serious and sincere evaluation of a company's operations by CEOs and key executives responsible for running the business of a homogeneous corporation or discrete divisions (business units) of a larger conglomerate. The authors wanted to make it an interesting experience, a fun exercise. That's why the self-audit is designed as a round of golf with pars, bogies and birdies. Each hole of the 18-hole golf course represents a key area for the success of the business. How is it played today? How should it be played tomorrow?

The authors hope that the evaluation doesn't stop with the calculation of the *score* and the computation of the *handicap* of one's company. The real objective is to stimulate interest, innovation and creativity to start new actions to run the business better. Management must become eager to reduce the handicap and consistently play better than par, at the top pro level, as a world-class operation.

The authors are genuinely interested in improving the level of management efficiency and helping to create better operating results for the practitioners of this *golfing* experience. We would like to establish an electronic, if not personal, dialogue to hear about the results of the *game* and its aftermath. Do not hesitate to use e-mail (Michael Kami: kami@icanect.net) or faxes (William Martz: 248-788-7862) to communicate with us. Give us your feedback, your criticisms, your feelings! We'll answer any questions you may have.

It's part of the fun process of writing, learning and growing to help executives in their quest for a better future!

We hope you enjoy reading this book and that you'll use it to improve your business.

Mike Kami and Bill Martz
Lighthouse Point, FL and Farmington Hills, MI

He that publishes a book runs a very great hazard, since nothing can be more impossible than to compose one that may secure the approbation of every reader.

Miguel de Cervantes (Don Quixote—1605)

ABOUT THE AUTHORS

Dr. Michael J. Kami was the chief strategic planner for two small companies that made good: IBM and Xerox during their super-growth years. He retired young and moved to Florida many years ago. But he couldn't just stand still. He became a one-man mini-conglomerate: a combination consultant, writer, public speaker, motorcycle rider, publisher, boatsman and entrepreneur. During the past ten years, he has served as a consultant on the board of directors of Harley-Davidson, during its successful transformation. He is considered one of the leading business advisers in the world and has been featured in many magazines and publications in the United States and abroad. He is knowledgeable, down-to-earth and tells it as it is. Peter Drucker and Tom Peters called him the best planner they know. His latest books, *Management Alert: Don't Reform, Transform!* and *Management Golf: What's Your Handicap?,* have become compulsory reading for managers. His quarterly publication *Kami Strategic Assumptions* provides timely advice to top executives in the United States and abroad.

William Martz specializes in the installation of management systems which include strategic planning, operational management, information systems and organization development. He holds A.B., M.B.A., and J.D. degrees.

He has worked with companies in a variety of industries, including service, manufacturing, retail and associations. His market focus has been on the so-called "non-Fortune 500" companies. His list of clients is diverse, ranging from the National Association of Securities Dealers to Eckrich Food Products. The nature of the service he provides is the application of the management process in real-life organizational situations. He uses a hands-on approach, not a consulting report and recommendation method. This approach includes regular monthly visits with clients, spread over a number of years, so that the clients can assimilate management principles and install them as best practices in their own organizations.

His service as president of companies in the manufacturing the information services industries has allowed him to offer practical experience, and not just theoretical knowledge. He has conducted public seminars in various parts of North and South America and has co-authored three books on the management process and strategic planning.

MANAGEMENT GOLF

SCORE CARD

Hole	Function	Par ⚑	Your Score	Diff. ✎	Observations/ Actions
1	Objectives	4			
2	Marketplaces	4			
3	Customer	3			
4	Product	5			
5	Competition	3			
6	Technology	4			
7	Strategy	4			
8	Management	5			
9	Organization	4			
10	Marketing	5			
11	Production	4			
12	Work	4			
13	People	4			
14	Systems	3			
15	Information	4			
16	Resources	5			
17	Finance	4			
18	Responsibility	3			
	Totals	72			

INTRODUCTION

Philosophy

The key thrust of this self-audit is a look at your business from the outside in! What are the environment's signals to the business for a better fit together? What are the market requirements the company must understand for higher mutual satisfaction? What are the customer needs and wants that must be fulfilled better by the company's products and services? What are the changing profiles of the employees, and are they being satisfied by the company's rewards and policies? Every question, every evaluation, every step must be viewed and acted upon from the outside in, never from the inside out. The company, the executives, everyone and everything in the business must adapt to the changing and challenging outside forces. That's the key to the present and future success of any organization. It's the basic and most important thrust of thinking and action for any organization.

Instructions

HOLE DESCRIPTION—The self-audit is designed to resemble a round of golf. Eighteen most important business factors have been carefully selected, representing the 18 holes on a golf course.

Management Golf: What's Your Handicap?

Hole	Par	Function	Hole	Par	Function
1	4	Objectives	10	5	Marketing
2	4	Marketplaces	11	4	Production
3	3	Customer	12	4	Work
4	5	Product/service	13	4	People
5	3	Competition	14	3	Systems
6	4	Technology	15	4	Information
7	4	Strategy	16	5	Resources
8	5	Management	17	4	Finance
9	4	Organization	18	3	Public responsibility
Σ	36	■ ■ ■ ■ ■	Σ	36	■ ■ ■ ■ ■ ■ ■

Each key subject is further subdivided into three, four or five sections, representing the number of strokes for par for each hole. The sections are shown at each hole.

HAZARDS—To make the exercise of self-audit more interesting and to add some zest to the process, course hazards are assigned appropriate names or caveats, representing common management errors, such as *lack of service* or *management apathy*. A graphic layout of each hole is shown at the end of each chapter.

SCORING—The scoring is just slightly more complex than in a real golf game. The following is an example of the scoring evaluation table which will be available for *each hole*. This example is for a ***par three*** hole.

Stroke Description	Hazard Description	BAD Double Bogey +2	SO/SO Bogey +1	GOOD Par 0	SUPER Birdie −1
First of three key criteria for critical evaluation by the executive playing the game.	Space for description of the *hazard*—negative influences on the business.			✓	
Second of three key criteria for critical evaluation by the executive playing the game.	Space for description of the *hazard*—negative influences on the business.		✓		
Third of three key criteria for critical evaluation by the executive playing the game.	Space for description of the *hazard*—negative influences on the business.				✓
Score on this hole **(below, above or at par)**		0 + 1 − 1 = 0 (PAR)			

Rate your company's performance on each of the individual items (three, four or five for each hole). Then add up your strokes to come up with your score for each hole. Enter the total for each hole on your overall score card to determine your overall performance against the par for each of the 18 holes. You can easily calculate what your company's overall handicap is against the par of 72 strokes on this corporate golf course. You may also want to use the blank scoring cells for bullet style notes to prompt innovative actions to solve problems and exploit opportunities.

Ratings

1. Rate your operation fairly, but conservatively. *Super-good* is an outstanding performance, world-class best! If you rate yourself *super-good* on too many items, you may end up with an incredibly low **negative** score for one or more holes. In that case, arbitrarily change your score for that hole to **1 (one),** indicating a *hole-in-one*. This is the only time you may have to fudge the scoring system. You can avoid this situation by becoming slightly more critical of or realistic about your performance and operation.

2. There may be some cases, hopefully very few, where a description of a *stroke* for a particular hole does not apply to your company's operations. Don't fret and don't try to force a score. Just mark it **0** (par) and continue your self-evaluation.

Note of Caution

When you read the PRO'S COMMENTS about the proper *strokes* for each hole of the management course, your immediate and natural reaction may be: These are well-known platitudes; everybody is aware of them—it's nothing new or different. It's *a firm grasp of the obvious*! Don't rush to these fast conclusions. Reflect on the success ratio of most companies, particularly in recent years. Why so many failures? Why so many mismanaged enterprises? Why so many mediocre results? Why so many shoddy products and services? The answer is simple. Too many companies are not managed well; too many managers don't follow the obvious!

After you compare your own operation against the self-evident platitudes about the various strokes, don't prejudge the golf course as too easy. Reevaluate your own swing carefully, honestly and critically. Compare your performance to other companies, competitors and noncompetitors. Do it on a global basis. Your revised final score may surprise you. It could also lead to many improvements in the way your organization is managed today.

Ask your associates to duplicate your efforts, play their own game and score as they see it. Compare the results. If there are many differences, ask yourself *why*. You may gain greater insight and broader objectivity. You will also clearly visualize many actions you can take or recommend to improve the company and its operations.

When a thought is too weak to be expressed simply,
it should be rejected.

Marquis de Luc Vauvenargues (1746)

PRO'S COMMENTS

1. VISION/MISSION—There's a great need for an objective attempt to try to describe the *vision* of the future, or external conditions within which the business will operate. While no one possesses a crystal ball, a scenario of the future environment (global, economic, social and political) provides a common base of reference and understanding. This base can and, in all probability, will be modified as real conditions and events diverge from the original assumptions. The scenario of the future must be evaluated at least once a year. It should be changed, if necessary, to reflect the best reality that can be mustered at each review. One should never operate with a vision of the future which has become obsolete or flawed by new and usually unpredicted events. This will inevitably happen and must be dealt with, *pronto*!

The mission of the business is what the company has decided to be in the future, within a scenario of the external environment outside of management's control. This is represented by the key objectives (quantitative and qualitative) describing the desired results.

It's good practice to provide additional explanation as to the rationale of any vision, mission and objectives statement. People want to know the reasons behind the *pronouncements*. They will not accept them blindly. They are entitled to a logical explanation of the philosophy and aims of the company in light of global change and new conditions of the future. Such demands may be hard to swallow for *old-fashioned* executives, but those are the new rules of our new society. Don't fight them. Embrace them!

2. SPECIFICITY—The objectives of the business must be clear, precise and unequivocal. They should demand superior performance within the context of the future conditions and the global competitive arena. They must be challenging but practically achievable. The time of hanging a carrot in front of the donkey is long gone. The set of objectives must embrace all critical phases of operations, from customer satisfaction to creative R&D, from speed of production to time compression of distribution, from desired financial results to defined social responsibility criteria. Objectives must be real and must be taken seriously. They're the desired target and provide the measurement criteria against actual results. Objectives are your *score card* parameters.

Avoid vagueness and generalizations. Statements that smack of platitudes, *motherhood* and *pie-in-the-sky* must be avoided. They're counterproductive because they lack the important sense of reality and don't provide the necessary handle for implementation. Ambiguity creates unnecessary divisiveness of opinions and leads to pointless and time-consuming discussions. Specificity is also important for testing prospective actions against a well-defined target.

3. CLEAR UNDERSTANDING—The specific and comprehensive objectives must be clearly understood by all managers and by all employees. In many cases, the understanding must be extended to suppliers, distributors, subcontractors and the community. There should be no mystery, no secrecy, no ambiguity about any of the objectives of the business. They should be well publicized and well explained. They also should be kept current and modified, if necessary, as external conditions change. It's important to provide a continuous flow of information about all the objectives to everyone concerned, directly or indirectly. Communications regarding objectives must be well thought out and well executed, in an honest, open and sincere manner.

A common mistake is to assume that vision, mission and objectives are well understood by the vast majority of personnel. In reality, most people, even in managerial positions, are usually unclear about the company's intended future direction. They don't take it seriously and believe that *what's for lunch* is more important than what's in the future.

4. CREDIBILITY—Communications must transmit believable messages. Are company objectives believed to be true by the people receiving the messages? Periodic tests must be conducted on whether managers and the employees consider objectives as an important guideline or mere company propaganda without substance. It's essential to provide full credibility to all parties concerned. Management must find out if some objectives are not considered real and why. The entire process of management will falter if pockets of doubt or lack of care exists in various parts of the business. The same applies to outsiders who need to believe that the company is serious and truthful about its objectives and goals.

The credibility of any statement for the future deteriorates rapidly during times of crisis. Typical vision statements, such as *people are our most important asset* and *the company highly respects the worth of every individual*, lose their credibility after the announcement of summary layoffs of 10 percent or more of the entire work force. The rebuilding of the morale takes much more than discredited good intentions printed on a piece of paper.

A common problem with corporate announcements which lack credibility is that many top managers still believe that they can get away with manipulation rather than truth and candor. Our society has become very sophisticated in its perception of what's true, what's a lie, what's propaganda and what's a half-truth. Corporate managers, public relations experts and politicians must become better attuned to the higher sensitivity, better perception and uncanny common sense of *ordinary* people. The same advice applies to the corporate lawyers who often act as censors of company announcements and pronouncements.

You see things, and you say "Why?"
But I dream things that never were; and I say "Why not?"

George Bernard Shaw (1930)

HOLE 1　　　OBJECTIVES　　　PAR 4

SCORING

	Stroke Description	Hazard Description	BAD Double Bogey +2	SO/SO Bogey +1	GOOD Par 0	SUPER Birdie −1
1	Our company has a clear, current scenario of the future environment and a complete set of up-to-date objectives for every phase of the business.	a) Mainly financial objectives. b) Haphazard or apathetic updating.				
2	Our scenarios and objectives are specific. They can be measured, compared and quantified for all activities of the business.	We practice: a) Vagueness. b) Generalities. c) *Motherhood* objectives.				
3	Our employees and outsiders have a clear and precise understanding of all objectives as they pertain to their performance.	a) Too much secrecy. b) Lack of communication. c) Lack of understanding.				
4	Our employees and outsiders genuinely believe that our objectives are challenging but fair. Management is not *playing games*!	a) Pattern of *say*, but not *do*. b) No consequences for lack of achievement. c) Acceptance of *excuses*.				

HOLE 1   OBJECTIVES   PAR 4

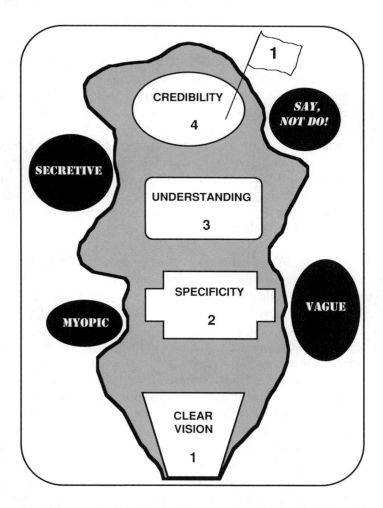

Where there is no vision, people perish.

Hebrew Bible (Proverbs 29:18)
quoted by President Kennedy
on the eve of his assassination

HOLE 2   MARKETPLACES   PAR 4

PRO'S COMMENTS

1. SPECIFIC MARKET NEEDS/WANTS—It's easy and fashionable to say *we're a market-driven company*. It's much more difficult to actually perform like one. Many companies that believe they are market driven describe the external market from their internal point of view. They analyze, often very thoroughly and analytically, the products and services they provide. There's always, however, a tendency to skew the feedback to our own offerings. That's *inside-out*.

True, unbiased market needs and wants must be determined on a continuous basis from the *outside-in*. What functions do the ***ideal*** products and services provide to fulfill the users' demanding expectations? It may often spell bad news for our offerings. That's genuine *outside-in*.

The above applies to existing, well-defined markets with proven, mature technologies, where the customers are accustomed to the products and services provided to them. The difficulty arises for very new, emerging technologies, where new possibilities are difficult to visualize and assess.

The customer may have a vague idea of the potential functions but no experience in the actual performance of the new products and/or services. In the latter case, conventional market research techniques, such as interviews, focus groups and questionnaires, are practically useless. A good example is the original forecast by IBM for its newly developed PC in 1982. The best IBM brains forecast a total world market for PCs of 200,000! IBM lost interest in pursuing such a small opportunity. Today, shipments of PCs exceed 200,000 a week! Around the same time, AT&T had an opportunity to acquire *free* permits and licenses to exploit the new cellular phone market. It forecast that the entire market for the service would be two million in 1995 and passed over the opportunity. Today, there are 20 million cellular subscribers in the United States alone! AT&T paid some $12 billion to acquire McCaw cellular service to reenter the market. It takes different techniques and different mentalities to understand and calculate more accurately the impact of new technologies on the relatively unimaginative general public.

2. PROSPECTS FOR GROWTH—The opportunity for growth in each market segment in which you are a player is a crucial question and requires a crucial determination. What is the future market potential for each segment? How is it changing? What are the main reasons: changing customer needs, changing technologies, changing economic and social circumstances, competing alternatives? The proper assessment of growth potential must be performed thoroughly, methodically and at regular intervals. There is always the danger of complacency, considering the situation static and taking it for granted. That's when surprises happen! Consider the immense shifts in the market segments of luxury cars, discount mass merchandising, pharmaceutical distribution channels, cruise ship construction, specialty magazine publishing and building materials specifications after a rash of hurricanes and earthquakes.

You must maintain comprehensive databases on all segments of your markets, present and future. The information must be global, even if the company is currently wholly domestic. Thorough knowledge of global markets is essential for assessing potential positive or negative changes to present markets because of the influx of foreign competitors, with different approaches, different technologies and different pricing.

3. MARKET ACTION PRIORITIES—No company, not even the world's biggest industrial giants, has enough resources to fund and pursue all possible avenues of worthy endeavor. The relevant word is: **priorities!** It's important to remember that there is no such thing as *allocation* of resources. There is only *reallocation* of always limited resources. The practice of proper allocation of people, time and money to one's various market segments is crucial to the success and often survival of the enterprise. The allocation is not always directly proportional to the reality of the market and its potential. Business executives are human and are prone to rationalize their personal likes and dislikes, promote their favorites, protect their turf and skew facts and figures to their psychological or power needs. Proper balance between the present and the future, between a stable but mature *golden goose* and a potential large and new but risky market, is a delicate and difficult decision. It must be made as objectively as possible.

4. EARLY DETECTION OF MARKET CHANGES—No market is static, and all work on any segment must be considered *transitory*. Market research should not be considered, nor performed, as a periodic function. It must become a continuous effort, inextricably woven into the mesh of information flow about the entire operation: sales, units, profits, costs, quality, acceptance, fluctuations. Any changes, often described as *deltas*, must be analyzed as to their reasons. Do they indicate a temporary, normal, seasonal blip or are they an early indication of a basic, fundamental market shift, down or up? The key is to establish a method for early detection of fundamental shifts—an early warning device, a *smell test*! A successful system for monitoring market shifts is not only absolutely necessary in today's fast-changing and often unpredictable environment, it's the best tool for protecting and enhancing the growth and prosperity of the enterprise. It should be accepted as one of the most important—in fact, vital—functions of the company, requiring full participation, cooperation and funding. By definition, early detection means better and faster availability and analysis of data. It requires information technology combined with brains!

With over 50 foreign cars already on sale here, the Japanese auto industry isn't likely to carve out a big slice of the U.S. market for itself.

The Wall Street Journal, August 2, 1968

HOLE 2   MARKETPLACES   PAR 4

SCORING

	Stroke Description	Hazard Description	BAD Double Bogey +2	SO/SO Bogey +1	GOOD Par 0	SUPER Birdie −1
1	We clearly identify and define all our markets and market segments. We analyze them from the customer point of view, without bias and and internal myopia.	a) Confusing familiarity about our customers' needs and wants. b) Lack of continuous, objective research of changes in each market.				
2	We thoroughly assess each of our market segments in its relation to the other segments. Objective priorities are set, according to our estimate of present and future value and rate of growth and contribution of each segment.	a) Resting on present success as a valid indication of the future. b) Inadequate market segmentation, with positives hiding negatives because of an excessively broad definition of each segment. Inadequate niche definition.				
3	We reallocate our resources of personnel, time and money to correspond to our market segment priorities, present and future.	a) *Generic* actions for all market segments: *one size fits all.* b) Favorites or sacred cows receive excessive amount of resources and top management attention.				
4	Our market research is a continuous effort based on steady, innovative collection of pertinent data for an up-to-date analysis of the situation.	Reliance on past knowledge and data, which may have become obsolete and misleading due to faster change in the marketplace.				

HOLE 2   MARKETPLACES   PAR 4

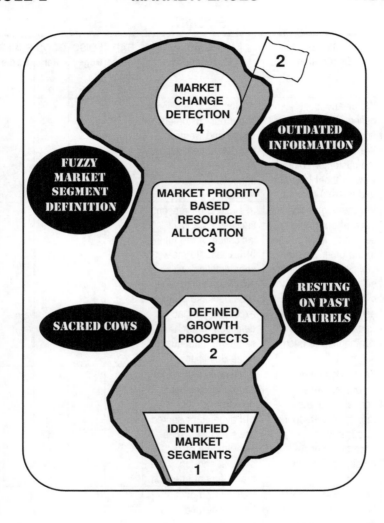

PRO'S COMMENTS

1. PRESENT CUSTOMERS—Present, live, revenue-producing customers must be the first priority of any organization. They are the *golden geese* who pay the daily bills. You must understand them, track them and *love* them! They may change their needs and wants slowly and subtly. You must be on top of the slightest hint of change. Even the smallest *delta* becomes large and significant with time. The sides of a small angle create a huge gap when they are extended far enough! Don't neglect small hints: be organized to detect them, catalog them, analyze them and act upon them. Your future existence depends on your present sensitivity.

Don't take any customer or class of customers for granted. There is no *eternal* loyalty. Customer loyalty is actually eroding faster than ever before, and immediate steps should be taken to stem any detected trend.

2. POTENTIAL CUSTOMERS—Ask yourself a key question: *Why isn't a particular potential customer our present customer*? You must consciously and critically evaluate your capabilities to satisfy customers' needs. You must do it continuously on a well-organized basis. Information must be solid, unbiased, significant and timely. Such a system must be given a high priority. It's the company's insurance policy for the longer range future. Flip-flop in your insistent questioning on how to keep present customers and gain new ones. Don't blame competition, the economy or the party in power. Blame yourself, constructively, and then act!

3. LIVING DATABASE—Today's computer technology provides all the necessary tools for the creation of a meaningful database on all present and potential customers. Programs, data collection and communications exist and can be immediately put to use. There's no excuse for not having a complete *dossier* on every individual customer or class of customers, with all the pertinent information to track individual history, sales, trends, progress or losses. The problem, in most cases, is not with the system. It's in the use of the system, proper attention, tracking and analysis. You must **believe** that it is a crucial part of your operation.

The same approach should be taken with potential customers, tracking their progress with competitive products and services. The same principle applies to all different types of businesses: consumer, industrial, transportation, etc.

Don't accept excuses. Insist that it's done and done well!

One set of messages of the society we live in is: Consume. Grow. Do what you want. Amuse yourselves. The very working of this economic system, which has bestowed these unprecedented liberties, most cherished in the form of physical mobility and material prosperity, depends on encouraging people to defy limits.

Susan Sontag (1989)

HOLE 3   CUSTOMERS   PAR 3

SCORING

	Stroke Description	Hazard Description	BAD Double Bogey +2	SO/SO Bogey +1	GOOD Par 0	SUPER Birdie −1
1	We anticipate the changing needs of our present customers. We adjust promptly and efficiently. We *love* our customers!	a) Intuitive familiarity rather than objective knowledge. b) Taking customers for granted!				
2	We know our potential customers well. We have excellent programs in place to convert them to become our customers.	a) Neglect of opportunities for potential new customers. b) Lack of research for expansion of customer base.				
3	We have an up-to-date database with all the necessary information on our present and potential customers.	Placing low priority on customer database systems and implementation.				

It may take months to find a customer, seconds to lose one.

Customers with bad experiences tell eleven people about it.
Those with good experiences tell only six.

Anon.

HOLE 3   CUSTOMERS   PAR 3

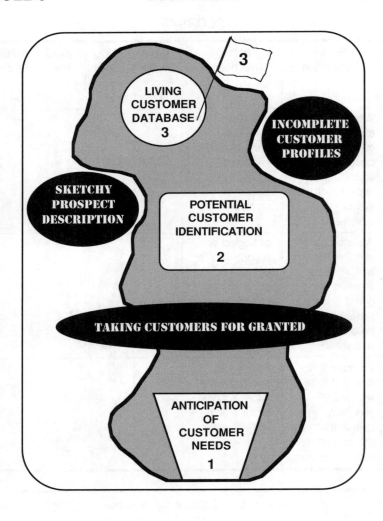

HOLE 4   PRODUCT/SERVICE   PAR 5

PRO'S COMMENTS

1. CUSTOMER SATISFACTION—Whoever uses your product or service has the right to expect that it will function as represented. The *satisfied* customer is not satisfied by prompt repairs or adjustments to make it right. The customer should be the main reason for doing it right the first time as an objective. The most complex technologies and systems must appear simple to the user. The user wants results, not explanations. Frequent and unbiased customer surveys are essential to assure objectivity in judging progress in achieving true customer satisfaction. Customers in all market segments—goods and services, consumer and industrial—have become more knowledgeable and more demanding. The standard of satisfaction has risen. Don't compare the past to the present. Create new levels of performance in tune with the times.

2. PLEASING THE CUSTOMER—Delivering a product or service that is functionally operational is not enough to rank you at the top of the list of suppliers. You need to take another step—go the extra mile—to deliver additional benefits that make it easy and pleasant to do business with your company. It's a combination of small details like easy-to-read instructions, fast telephone access, prompt and intelligent replies to inquiries, no delay in providing replacement parts, willingness to listen to *trivia* and a sincere smile. You succeed when the customer says that *you really care*! Add an additional *soft touch* to your handling of customers. It's much needed to alleviate the growing feeling of alienation that results from customers having to talk to answering machines which instruct them to press buttons and to perform tasks benefiting the seller, not the buyer.

3. COMPETITIVE DIFFERENTIATION—Successful companies carry on their business in a way that's positively different from the competition, and they get noticed for it: Nordstrom for personal service in department stores and Hewlett-Packard for reliability of its computer products. A major insurance company's reputation for the poor handling of customers' claims is obviously a negative differentiation, competitors look excellent in comparison.

Conversations about people revolve around their personalities: nice or nasty, reliable or nonreliable, straightforward or manipulative. The same happens with companies. Customers and noncustomers talk about the personality of a company. This word-of-mouth assessment flows throughout the market area, like gossip. A successful company needs *nice* things said about it. It doesn't matter whether it's a consumer or industrial enterprise. It's important to determine the market's psychological opinion about yourself and how it compares to the competition. It's not a question of a *me too* imitation. It's a willful attempt at positive differentiation from the pack. It goes beyond product/service quality and performance. You want the market to have a *good feeling* about your company. Fortune's *Most Admired Corporations* list shows how fast ratings can change. Previously successful giants, consistently rated among the ten most admired, have fallen to the 300–400 ranking of least admired in a span of two years.

4. CRITICAL SELF-ANALYSIS—The traditional evaluation of a company's strengths and weaknesses is accepted as a given and is a must in any organization. In reality, it's often a perfunctory planning exercise which is either routinely included among masses of other material or stated in broad generalities that lead to little or no action. A truly critical evaluation of all facets of operations dealing with the customer is essential for continuous improvement of the organization. It requires proper motivation of all employees to state their opinions forcefully and honestly. These must be sorted, evaluated and agreed upon, in order of priority, for active implementation. The key element in such an evaluation is to achieve genuine objectivity and accurate statement of facts. Internal admission of inadequacies is difficult. It requires a positive and nonpunitive attitude by top management to encourage frankness.

5. PRODUCT/SERVICE *PRODUCTIVITY*—Fast changes in technology and market demand create fast obsolescence of products and services. Continuous monitoring of the **value** of every one of your products and services is imperative on a global basis. This applies to the price/performance ratio in all categories of your offerings to the customer. Customers are interested in the bottom-line performance of their purchases. Detailed effort is needed to keep up to date and to juggle technological features, quality, reliability, performance and price for the mutual benefit of the customer and the company. While it's essential, it's also very difficult. Optimizing is never easy, but today's complexity of balancing the many inputs and options is often beyond analysis. It requires an intuitive *smell test* to arrive at the proper timing and the correct balance of technology and price.

1. As a customer, you are entitled to be treated like a real individual, feeling human being...with friendliness, honesty and respect.
2. You are entitled to full value for your money.
3. You are entitled to a complete guarantee of satisfaction.
4. You are entitled to fast delivery.
5. You are entitled to speedy, courteous, knowledgeable answers on inquiries.
6. You are entitled to be an individual dealing with other individuals.
7. You are entitled to all the help we can give in finding exactly the product or information you need.
8. You are entitled to be treated exactly as we want to be treated when we are someone else's customer.

Summary of the Customers' Bill of Rights
adopted by the Quill Corporation in **1970!**

HOLE 4   PRODUCT/SERVICE   PAR 5

SCORING

	Stroke Description	Hazard Description	BAD Double Bogey +2	SO/SO Bogey +1	GOOD Par 0	SUPER Birdie −1
1	Our company's products and services are high quality and customer oriented.	Lack of objectivity in determining quality and ease of use from the customer's viewpoint.				
2	All our employees perform and treat the customers as they would like to be treated.	*Customer comes first* is lip-service and an empty slogan.				
3	Our company has established a very positive image and reputation in the marketplace.	We rank below our competition in the market perception of customer orientation.				
4	Our company *ego attachment* to our product/service has been deflated to objectively look at ourselves from the customer viewpoint.	a) Emotional attachment to the successful product/service line. b) Danger of delaying new lines to protect the present.				
5	Our product/service provides the latest and best performance/price ratio to our customers. We adapt fast to state-of-the-art and price balance in all our lines.	a) Stretching design and service past their life span to milk the last ounce of profit. b) Comparing our product/service to the average, not the global leader.				

HOLE 4   PRODUCT/SERVICE   PAR 5

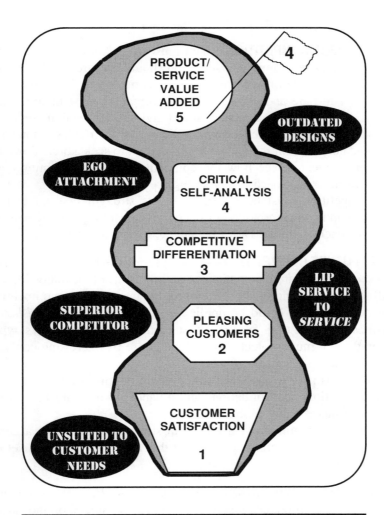

The consumer is our boss, quality is our job
and value for money is our goal.

Quality Principle of Mars, Inc.

HOLE 5　　　COMPETITION　　　PAR 3

PRO'S COMMENTS

1. DIRECT COMPETITION—You must try to know your competitors as well as you know yourself. You should prepare a strategic and operational profile of every one of your competitors; it should be in depth, up to date and accurate. The information must include their financial history; the sequence, speed and success of their product/service introduction; their pricing policies and their sales compensation and commission schedules. It's important to seek a breakdown by market segment to see how the competition is differentiating each segment in its approach to marketing.

Competition must be classified by its strength in each market segment and compared to your own relative position. Ask the reasons why for each segment. Don't be satisfied with generalities.

2. FUTURE COMPETITION—Make a serious stab at preparing various scenarios of future potential competition. One of the major sources will be new technologies, developed by presently noncompetitive businesses, which could be applied to make your *bread-and-butter* business obsolete (e.g., plastics vs. steel, desktop publishing vs. typesetting). You must protect your golden goose by exercising constant technological vigilance.

Another major wave of serious competition may arise from mergers, acquisitions, consolidations and alliances, which are both common and increasingly global.

You must continuously update your strategies and actions according to the early warning signals from the *intelligence* sources set up by your company.

3. COMPETITIVE PRODUCT/SERVICE EVALUATION—Whatever your business, product or service, whether consumer or industrial, construction or mining, you must prepare a detailed, objective comparison of each product/service unit or model on the market. How does it compare in price, quality, performance, features, systems, serviceability, packaging, delivery and scope vs. every one of your own offerings. Obviously, you want an impartial, unbiased, even strongly critical evaluation. You also want to conduct analyses on a continuous, planned basis to detect positive and negative shifts. These *deltas* are the most important input for key decisions and offensive or defensive actions on your part.

In many instances, the biggest difficulty is intellectual honesty. Many companies refuse to accept factual data that competitors' products have many superior features. On the surface, such a statement may sound ridiculous, yet *psychological myopia* is very prevalent, particularly among the highest-ranking executives of larger businesses. You must break through the barrier of stubborn self-satisfaction and resistance to change. Fight for continuous improvements to your products and services. It is the only way to ensure a better future for your organization.

There are two kinds of companies:
those that are competitive and those that are closed.

Anon.

HOLE 5   COMPETITION   PAR 3

PRO'S COMMENTS

	Stroke Description	Hazard Description	BAD Double Bogey +2	SO/SO Bogey +1	GOOD Par 0	SUPER Birdie −1
1	We have specific and detailed profiles of all our competitors. We identify their characteristics and unique profiles.	We underestimate the strength and progress of our global competitors.				
2	Our competition information base clearly identifies different and emerging technologies that could have direct impact on our markets.	a) We are unfamiliar with technologies that *appear* unrelated to our business. We don't pry in depth. b) We are complacent about early warnings that may affect our products or services.				
3	Our competitive analysis laboratory continually analyzes in depth all our competitors' products and services. The reports are objective, competent and comprehensive. They are taken very seriously and vigorously acted upon.	a) Reliance on superficial analysis and gut feeling. b) Rationalizing deficiencies by offsetting strengths instead of tackling the problem directly.				

HOLE 5   COMPETITION   PAR 3

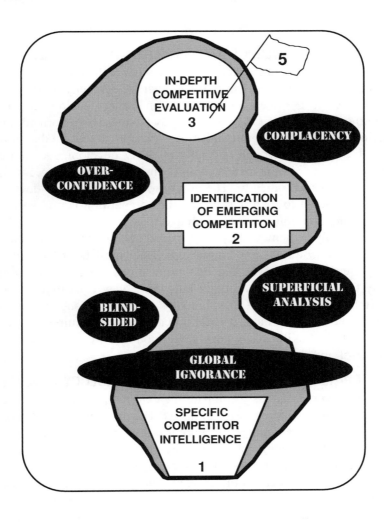

PRO'S COMMENTS

1. WORLD KNOWLEDGE ACCESSIBILITY—Data, information and knowledge are growing at an astonishing exponential rate. The growth is global and all-encompassing. It's crucial for company personnel to have access to the latest technological and other developments that will affect products, services and the way business is performed (production, distribution, communication). Computerized databases are available in all developed and also in many developing countries. Every company must prepare a comprehensive knowledge-access plan and follow it methodically. The ability to learn about new developments and adapt to them faster than the competition is probably the most significant competitive advantage today.

It can only be achieved by very special people, with a passion for finding and acquiring new knowledge. They must be trained in the latest electronic retrieval and communications system. They must apply the technology in a highly innovative way to search for new information, pertinent to the company's future, among billions of bytes of nonrelevant data. It's not an easy task. It requires imagination, analytical skills and a keen perception to differentiate between the useful and the interesting.

2. CRITICAL ANALYSIS OF COMPANY TECHNOLOGY—Every enterprise must continuously compare the external progress of relevant technology to its internal use and needs. The assessment must be all-encompassing: evaluation of technology that produces products and services and evaluation of technology that supports all operations needed to produce and market the company business. Marketing uses sophisticated feedback from scanned data of consumer purchases. Production is enhanced by complex programming of robotic machinery. Finance requires worldwide communications and electronic exchange of funds and currencies. Sales personnel need long-distance access to inventory, price and delivery information for immediate on-line quotes to their prospective customers. Strategic selection of one's technical expertise vs. the competition is crucial to success.

It's not enough to keep informed about changes in technology and rapidly occurring breakthroughs and developments. A company's future must be protected by some active participation in the process. A company must decide on a formula for regular, methodical, yearly investment in R&D. A percentage of total revenue or specific sales is probably the simplest and most often used criterion. It must be kept up in good times and bad. The latter is obviously a problem. IBM used to spend over $5 billion yearly on R&D. Recently, its R&D budget was pared down to $3.6 billion. That's an immense cut of some $2 billion annually. It helps the current profit picture, but how will it affect IBM's future, assuming that the draconian cuts aren't all deadwood, waste and overhead? Whatever your company's size, there should be an allocation for R&D. A relatively small metal bottle-cap producer with $20 million in sales invented and received a most valuable patent for a plastic cap replacement, upstaging billion-dollar giants like Alcoa, Reynolds Aluminum and Crown Cork.

3. EMERGING NEW TECHNOLOGIES—Two areas must be tracked in technology. The first and obvious one relates to present business and present operations. The second consists of new and emerging technologies, particularly when they are very different from the company's traditional know-how. Kodak was basically a chemical company with tremendous investment in film (silver halide) technology. Top management ignored for too long the impact of electronic imaging, which eventually will make chemical film obsolete. The board of directors finally removed Kodak's *chemical* top management and replaced it with an *electronic* team, with Mr. Fisher, formerly with Motorola, as CEO. The move should have been made eight years sooner!

There are three roads to ruin: women, gambling and technicians. The most pleasant is with women, the quickest is with gambling, but the surest is with technicians.

Georges Pompidou, French President (1968)

The lesson is not to fall in love with a technology but rather with the final output of any technology: a product or service that responds to a market need. The technology must be a slave to the market need, not its master! It should also be promptly discarded when it no longer satisfies customers' needs. That's a most difficult task for single-technology-dependent companies threatened with competition from new branches of knowledge alien to their traditional discipline.

4. ROUTES TO TECHNOLOGY—The *do-it-all-yourself* concept has been replaced by the policy of *sharing*. Companies license technologies, exchange them, and form joint research and development teams. In many cases, large transnationals jointly develop complex components (particularly in the electronic chip area) and then fiercely compete with each other in marketing consumer or industrial products that contain the jointly developed parts. Each company must redefine its policies on in-house vs. external procurement of technologies. The policy of sharing has become a must because of the cost and complexity of doing everything alone. The new balance is difficult to formulate. It must be done very carefully and very diplomatically to keep up the morale of in-house development personnel. At the same time, communication and the exchange of ideas with other organizations on a worldwide basis must be stimulated. Another approach, gaining popularity, is to outsource research and development of new technologies to organizations specializing in such endeavors as their main business. It's an outgrowth of the contract research by universities and foundations and is now done on a global scale. The negative is the lack of control over the outcome of such outsourcing. Realistically, however, there's not much control over timing and results of pioneering research efforts performed in one's own laboratories.

Art is the beautiful way of doing things. Science is the effective way of doing things. Business is the economic way of doing things.

Elbert Hubbard (1921)

HOLE 6　　　　TECHNOLOGY　　　PAR 4

SCORING

	Stroke Description	Hazard Description	BAD Double Bogey +2	SO/SO Bogey +1	GOOD Par 0	SUPER Birdie −1
1	We are extremely sensitive to the explosion of world knowledge. We have access to and use global databases in all departments affected by technological change.	a) We are large and powerful enough to do it alone (e.g., IBM). b) We are too small to afford global database access.				
2	Our personnel is open-minded and thirsty for new knowledge and technologies. We have eliminated the NIH (not invented here) syndrome. We budget and support our R&D efforts.	a) Resistance to new technologies and major changes of disciplines. b) NIH syndrome has not been eradicated. It just went underground. c) We cut our R&D budget to help the short-term profit picture.				
3	We are alert to emerging technologies, even far removed from our present expertise.	Myopic view (tunnel vision) about any competitor to our established technology.				
4	Our company is actively participating in sharing, exchanging and licensing new technologies.	a) We maintain a policy of excessive secrecy and confidentiality about our technology. b) We don't trust partners, alliances and joint ventures.				

HOLE 6   **TECHNOLOGY**   PAR 4

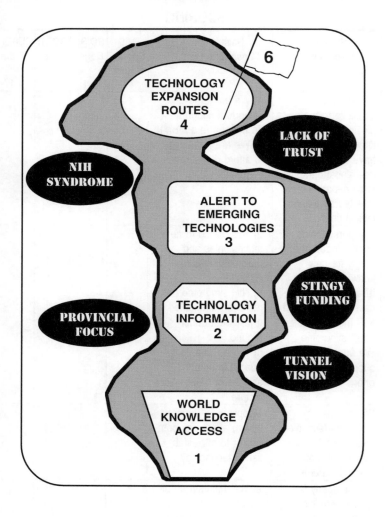

HOLE 7   STRATEGY   PAR 4

PRO'S COMMENTS

1. SELECTION—Objectives determine the destination, the *finish line*; strategy determines the route. The challenges along that route are facts and data gathered about *marketplaces* (Hole 2), *customers* (Hole 3), *products/services* (Hole 4), *technology* (Hole 5) and *competition* (Hole 6). Based on this information, you can choose the best itinerary to lead you across the desired finish line. It's a selection among many possible alternatives. The alternative routes are many and often almost equally attractive. But a choice must be made. Hesitation and lack of firm direction are major obstacles to successful travel to your destination. Strategy does not consist of detailed action steps. It's a broad course of action to address outside factors, not under your control, that may affect the opportunity to meet your objectives. Strategy is a combination of creative, insightful and wise decisions, based on correct and relevant information.

The concept of business strategy evolved from millennia of military procedures (e.g., *objective*: capture town X; *strategic alternatives*: (1) precision artillery shelling, (2) massive air bombardment, (3) cut off supplies). After the primary strategic selection is made, proper resources must be mustered and applied: cannons, airplanes or road and river blockades. Detailed action plans (logistics) must be drawn to carry out the selected alternative.

While the objectives of many companies may be very similar, the strategy for achieving them will often be the differentiating factors which lead to the success of one and the mediocrity or downfall of another. Strategy is not necessarily a brilliant and complex stroke of genius. More often, it's a *common-sense* approach that parallels the needs of the changing outside environment. The strategy of Wal-Mart, based on *lowest price* to the consumer, defeated the Kmart strategy, based on *broader product selection.* Consumers' rising budget constraints have dominated purchasing decisions during the past eight years. Wal-Mart's phenomenal growth left Kmart far behind and almost fatally wounded. Another vital element to strategy is timing. Identifying the right strategy for the right action at the right time is not easy. Many corporations are too late, but many are too early (e.g., Chrysler's aerodynamic car design of the sixties, AT&T's video telephone of the seventies and Sony's high-resolution Betamax of the eighties).

   2. EXTERNAL ROUTES—A market-driven philosophy (from outside-in) offers various broad routes for the overall direction of a business: (1) further penetration of present markets with present products—opportunity from further market growth, (2) expansion into additional markets (e.g., international) with present product/service lines, (3) expansion of present niche-market dabbling into major business segments through additional/different marketing and/or product/service improvement, (4) change or diversification into new markets with new products/services.

   Within each route there are many variations and fine-tuning choices. It's very important, however, to decide upon one major, dominant thrust, even if pursuing several parallel paths. Strategic directions within a company must be assigned clear priorities for allocation of limited resources and maintaining a sense of continuity.

   3. INTERNAL ROUTES—Internal needs must be decided upon only after reaching a clear decision about the direction and priorities of the *external* routes. You have to determine what competencies, skills, tools, systems, finances and other key resources are required to carry out the *outside-in* strategies. The two main strategic routes are *internal development* and *external acquisition* of required resources. While this may seem obvious, many companies don't have a clear understanding or don't follow a clear path based on these seemingly *simplistic* criteria. The outside acquisition of resources is gaining broad popularity because of the potential compression of time to get ready. The obvious negative is a certain loss of control over the outsider's implementation and compliance with mutually agreed upon terms and specifications. However, many managers forget that internal programs, theoretically completely under their control, also often stray widely from the timetable, from the budget and from expected/projected results.

4. FLEXIBILITY—It's important to follow a policy of flexibility and keep an open mind to potential changes in strategies. We do it with all other functions and operations, because of today's era of fast change and unpredictability. But we are often reluctant to change or adjust objectives and strategies. That's because, in the past, they were considered sacrosanct, a *given* to be accomplished, not to be tampered with. Today, strategies have to be regularly reviewed, reexamined and critically reevaluated as conditions and the external environment change and fluctuate drastically. It's important to follow a sequence of thought and actions. First, examine the implementation of programs and make necessary corrections. Second, reexamine the strategy and modify, if necessary. Third and always last, reevaluate the objectives as to their feasibility under the new external conditions. Change in objectives must be the last step in management's orderly review, but it may be a very necessary action.

It must be made clear throughout the organization that changes in strategies and objectives are not *shameful.* They should not be perceived as *negative* acts or admissions of failure. Change in direction should be viewed as a positive acknowledgment that management recognized, in time, important new trends. These require, in turn, a rapid adaptation of the business to new conditions. Such a proactive policy and attitude creates a positive atmosphere and encourages flexibility of thought and action among all personnel at management and worker levels.

Being good in business is the most fascinating kind of art...Making money is art and working is art and good business is the best art.

Andy Warhol, U.S. pop artist (1928–87)

HOLE 7   STRATEGY   PAR 4

SCORING

	Stroke Description	Hazard Description	BAD Double Bogey +2	SO/SO Bogey +1	GOOD Par 0	SUPER Birdie −1
1	We have well-defined, innovative strategies to support our objectives. These strategies guide our actions and programs.	a) Our managers don't have a clear understanding of our strategies. b) There's confusion between strategies and programs.				
2	Our strategies are based on the *outside-in* principle. They reflect the reality and the changes in the external markets.	Our external strategies have not been clearly prioritized for proper allocation of scarce resources.				
3	We have clearly defined all the resources needed for the implementation of our objectives through our strategies and programs—external and internal.	There's a lot of confusion and lack of consensus on what programs should be done in-house and which should be farmed out.				
4	Our management is alert to changes and is always willing to re-examine all strategies, if the circumstances warrant such steps.	Certain strategies have become *sacred cows.* Managers are even reluctant to bring some subjects up for discussion.				

HOLE 7 **STRATEGY** PAR 4

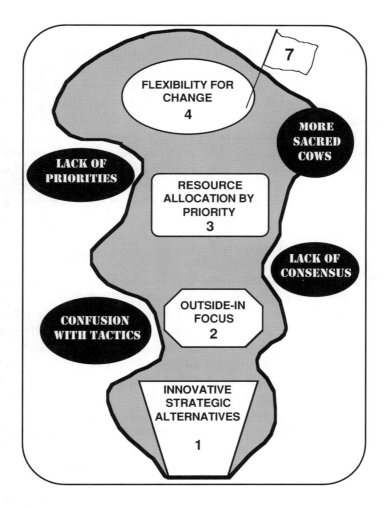

The propensity to truck, barter and exchange one thing for another is common to all humans and to be found in no other race of animals.

Adam Smith in *Wealth of Nations* (1776)

PRO'S COMMENTS

1. PROFESSION/DISCIPLINE—It used to be that management was considered to be the aggregate of the people who ran the company, the *bosses*. Emerson's saying—*an institution is the lengthened shadow of one man*—does not fit the modern world anymore. Good corporate management is now a discipline, a profession, a codified set of practices—as in law, medicine and architecture. The major components of the discipline of management are planning, implementation of plans and control of results. It's a structure that is similar to models in any other profession. It also leaves plenty of room and opportunities for creativity, imagination and nonconventional thinking. Management is carried out by managers: professionals responsible for using the latest available practices and techniques to try to make the best possible decisions for the benefit of the entire organization.

2. SCOPE AND STYLE—Only the CEO is responsible for the total organization as an entity. All other managers have partial areas of responsibility. These must be clearly and precisely identified. Both gaps and overlaps create inefficiency, confusion and dangerous delays in decisions and implementation. Precise definition of authority and responsibility is required for all the members of an organization, particularly in times of empowerment. It also applies to teams and partners (alliances, subcontractors, agents). In a dynamic organization, rapid response to changing conditions, greater flexibility of movement and self-initiative increase, rather than decrease, the need for continuous communication of people's scope of responsibility and authority. Failure to do so creates confusion and mismanagement.

Every company has a distinct *style* of management. It stems, in part, from its philosophy and also from the external circumstances such as the culture of the country in which one operates. The internal situation is an important determinant of style. It's easier to be participative when business and profits boom. Losses and decline bring about authoritative *crisis* style. As the old adage says, *the boss isn't always right, but he is always the boss.*

While broad generalizations are dangerous, businesses in most parts of the world are moving toward the *participative* management style. The reason is mostly cultural: people don't want to be bossed around in a dictatorial manner. The inner resentment creates lower productivity, lack of interest, disregard for quality and service and even deliberate sabotage, often on the production line. Participative style—empowering employees at all levels to communicate, suggest, innovate and think—is difficult to implement but brings superior results. Team concept, continuous improvement, total quality management and reengineering don't have to be slogans and half-baked *follow-the-crowd* attempts. They can be real and highly productive.

3. DELEGATION—Definitions of scope of responsibilities can be useless and actually antiproductive, unless the words are truly implemented and become an organizational way of life. Delegation, under empowerment, isn't telling a subordinate what and how to do something. It means encouraging successive lower levels of the organization to exercise their minds, talents, experience and creativity to do a better job in all endeavors. Successfully pushing delegation down the ranks will speed up reaction and response time, essential elements of success in an environment that thrives on time compression. Delegation doesn't and shouldn't mean abdication. Continuous and rapid feedback of results is as essential as delegation itself. The process is a closed loop of a self-reinforcing communication network linking all employees in their quest for a common goal of success.

4. DECISION FLEXIBILITY—Today's era of unpredictability means that no organization can forecast the future, even a short period ahead. Given these conditions, the key word for management is *flexibility*— flexibility of objectives, flexibility of strategies, flexibility of plans, flexibility of decisions and flexibility of implementation. Flexibility is the most important style of management. It's also disturbing to conventional executives, particularly those who were very successful in the past. They followed a very *deterministic* style of thought and action. What is is and will be! Today, there's need for a *probabilistic* approach. What is probably is and may or may not be in the future.

Remember when a company's long-term goals and objectives were set in concrete and considered immutable givens? Today, everything is flexible and could be changed, negotiated or even abandoned. An anonymous sage with a sense of humor pontificated that *forecasting is very difficult, particularly when it deals with the future.*

5. MONITORING—Continuous tracking of performance is obviously a major, probably a primary, requirement of responsible management. It's essential that executives, managers and everyone involved in decision making keep a steady hand on the *pulse of the enterprise.* New conditions make this platitude more difficult than one may think because of a paradox of technology. The latest advances in computers, electronic communication, scanning and on-line databases provide so much information that culling the important from the unimportant is a major and very difficult task. It's also imperative that such analysis be done and reviewed often. Many companies have established an executive key measurement briefing. It requires the selection of a limited number of most important factors related to the company's operations and keeping them up to date and immediately available for any manager's retrieval and review.

Surround yourself with the best people you can find,
delegate authority, and don't interfere.

Ronald Reagan (1986)

HOLE 8   MANAGEMENT   PAR 5

SCORING

	Stroke Description	Hazard Description	BAD Double Bogey +2	SO/SO Bogey +1	GOOD Par 0	SUPER Birdie −1
1	We have consciously chosen a style of management that fits the market environment and our strategic direction We are truly professional and up to date with management science.	a) Top management style conflicts with strategy and lower echelon practices. b) We confuse *power* with right decision making.				
2	Each manager's area of responsibility is clearly defined and understood. Overlapping areas are addressed cooperatively. We practice participative management.	a) Assuming, rather than ascertaining, that every manager understands his/her responsibilities. b) Assuming that clear definitions lead to clear implementation.				
3	Our delegation of power is consistent with our management style.	a) *Do* orders are confused with delegation. b) Monitoring actions instead of monitoring results.				

HOLE 8   **MANAGEMENT**   **PAR 5**

SCORING

	Stroke Description	Hazard Description	BAD Double Bogey +2	SO/SO Bogey +1	GOOD Par 0	SUPER Birdie −1
4	We have a built in flexibility that allows us to quickly adapt management style to changing outside conditions.	a) Systems are too rigid. b) Failure to empower decisions to lower levels impedes true *grassroots* policies.				
5	Our reporting system is as close to on-line and in real time as necessary.	We have a post-facto monitoring: too late for required fast reaction.				

True partnership is not:
And so we plough along, as the fly said to the ox.

Henry Wadsworth Longfellow (1840)

HOLE 8　　　　　**MANAGEMENT**　　　　**PAR 5**

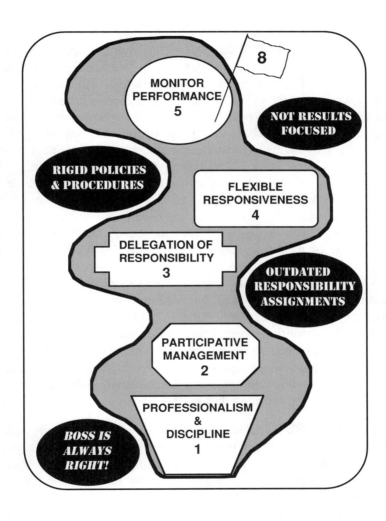

PRO'S COMMENTS

1. FUNDAMENTAL PHILOSOPHY—Underlying every action taken by an organization is its basic philosophy or set of beliefs. A business philosophy is different from the mission or nature of the business. The latter relates directly to the marketplace. However, the philosophy will shape the mission. It also constitutes the foundation for setting corporate policies, which, in turn, shape operating and working rules. In a way, a fundamental business philosophy is a statement of the personal values of the organization, set by the top management. The range can be very broad, from major ethical behavior to the dress code. It's important that the philosophy be clearly stated and thoroughly understood. The key words are *consistency* and *unequivocal.* Unless it is so, you invite misunderstandings, arguments, hassles and delays. All of these are harmful and costly. They slow down or impede vital decision making.

Yet, in today's era of fast change, even fundamental philosophies must be periodically reviewed. No subject should be considered *taboo*; no policy should be carved in granite to withstand the challenge of time. The more fundamental the subject, the more care and attention should be placed on its definition and its redefinition. Boards of directors and top management officers have a duty and a responsibility to define, review and enforce a fundamental, viable and ethical philosophy for the business that has been entrusted to their care.

2. STRUCTURE—The statement *structure follows strategy* may sound simple, yet it's very true and very profound. If the right structure is not in place, high performance in implementation of strategy is greatly reduced. In the *good old days,* most corporations followed a military organization structure. It was further based on functional competence rather than market performance. The underlying strategy was based on bottom-line performance and return on investment. It was an inside-out environment.

Today, survival and success depend on an overall outside-in strategy. It must be, however, further refined to determine which key outside elements are dominant: market breadth and vast distribution network, broad product line excellence, personal service orientation or technology-driven state-of-the-art impact. Each different emphasis will result in a different internal structure.

The concept of an *outside-in* dictated structure becomes more complex for corporations with many different businesses and/or when operating on a global basis. The proper structure of each division or operating unit may be quite different because the outside forces are different. Thus, divisional organizations shouldn't be forced to adopt a common structure under the corporate umbrella for the sake of uniformity and the aim for a *single* policy. The acceptance of diversity will create internal problems and even conflicts—different salary and benefits levels, different promotion and cross-divisional transfer criteria, different outsourcing and procurement policies, different pricing formulas, etc. The proper decision is to preserve the *outside-in* priority above the corporate *umbrella* uniformity.

Many organizations are concerned about the number of reporting levels and wish to reduce the traditional hierarchy. Here again, *outside-in* should prevail. What's the most efficient form of internal organization to satisfy the customer? It may be different for each business unit, but it will have some common characteristics—the least number of levels; the most empowerment for people down the decision ladder; the highest level of knowledge, proficiency and self-determination for every member of the organization; the most integrated, comprehensive, dynamic workflow process.

3. COMMUNICATION—This is a broad, difficult, frustrating field with myriad possibilities and pitfalls. Yet it must be tackled, tamed and managed. Major improvement of communication (down, up and across organizational lines) is essential to speed up decision making and actions in an era of time compression and the need for faster throughput.

We must distinguish between two main areas: (1) the physical means of message transmission and (2) the content of the message. Attractive and touted technology made the means dominant over the content. Obviously that's wrong. The real challenge in communication is the sender, whether a human or a database. Content must come first. GIGO—garbage in, garbage out—was coined a long time ago, but it's even more valid today.

4. COMPLEXITY: *KEEP IT SIMPLE, STUPID!* (KISS)—Application of Pareto's law to communication would probably show that 80 percent of what's being communicated is unimportant and could be eliminated to emphasize and clarify the 20 percent that's constructive and worthwhile. Simplification of databases, reports, input and output requirements, procedures and red tape would reduce bureaucracy, clarify the message and focus everyone's attention on the important, not the trivial. That's common sense. It's a lot to ask for because *common sense is very uncommon*, as stated by Plutarch in 51 B.C., paraphrased by Voltaire in 1756 and still valid today. As another old saying goes: *I wrote you a long letter, because I had no time to write you a short one!* We must all become communication specialists to help reduce the clutter, babble and obfuscation of business information. *Simplicity is not simple!* In fact, it's very, very difficult.

Every organization should launch a special campaign to fight bureaucracy and strangling procedures. Today's emphasis on time compression is in direct conflict with the *green eyeshade* mentality of *professional* bureaucrats. They're a menace to progress and to profits.

Early to bed, early to rise, work like hell and organize!

Albert Gore, Jr. (1988)

HOLE 9   ORGANIZATION   PAR 4

SCORING

	Stroke Description	Hazard Description	BAD Double Bogey +2	SO/SO Bogey +1	GOOD Par 0	SUPER Birdie −1
1	Our fundamental philosophy and basic set of values are precisely stated. They are understood and adhered to by all managers.	a) Assumption that our philosophy is really understood and accepted. b) Assumption that it actually guides decisions and actions at lower levels.				
2	Our organizational structure is flexible and based on outside-in strategies. These are clear, prioritized and well understood.	Confusing organization chart blocks and lines with real relationships and decision making.				
3	Efforts to improve communications within and outside our organization are continuous and of highest priority.	a) Excessive focus on mechanics rather than content. b) Lack of valid data to communicate.				
4	KISS is our motto, and we are winning the battle of simplicity.	Techno-babble is gaining in popularity!				

HOLE 9   ORGANIZATION   PAR 4

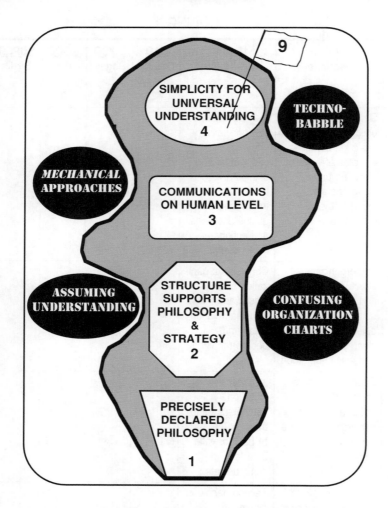

Why make it simple,
when you can easily make it very complicated?
Old German proverb

HOLE 10 MARKETING PAR 5

PRO'S COMMENTS

1. GUIDANCE—A market-driven company needs to bring the *outside* world into the *inside* operations. Acting as a sensor of the external environment and new opportunities is a key responsibility of marketing departments. *Market-driven* must be the key philosophy of doing business. It will not just happen by executive edict or by proclaiming the right platitudes. It must be a continuous and serious effort to constantly check the reality of the marketplace. It also means continuously evaluating the dynamics of external change on internal objectives, strategies, plans and programs.

2. OPPORTUNITY IDENTIFICATION—Changes in the marketplace deal not only with the present wants and needs of various customers and prospects in the markets. They must also consider the less obvious expectations and hidden desires. These are often vague definitions of different products and services. These are also *conveniences* in dealing with your company. The list is long: personal courtesies, delivery cycle time, credit approvals, electronic interfaces, easy access to knowledgeable representatives, ways of handling complaints, special accommodations for exceptions. A market-driven company listens for the purpose of positive differentiation. This will result in wider sales and, hopefully, greater profitability. Marketing may not be the ultimate decider, but it must act as an *ombudsman*, a caring representative of customer needs to the whole organization.

3. PRODUCT—The product/service is what you offer customers to satisfy them. When you run the product/service through the marketing function, you must look at it from a customer's viewpoint. Product/service characteristics must change to conform to the needs/wants of the marketplace. The marketing function must go from the outside to the inside to generate the input so that the product/service promptly adapts to the market needs. It then requires a change of direction back to the outside to show the customers that their wishes were heard and satisfied.

4. PRICING—It's evident that price is an economic and an emotional consideration of the customer and the customer only. It's not a cost-plus consideration of the seller or supplier. Yet, in too many cases, the inside-out pricing based on costs, not demand, dominates the marketing of products/services of many companies. During the eighties it was called the *American disease* or shotgun marketing vs. Japan's precise rifle micromarketing. During the nineties, U.S. outside-in marketing improved greatly and Japan's performance deteriorated somehow, but it is still world-class with Japan's awesome positive trade balance performance.

5. FUNCTIONAL OPERATIONS—In addition to being the sensor and guide to the outside world, the marketing function performs important activities, directly related to increasing sales of the organization. Four major categories should be addressed:

a. Personal Selling—The traditional evaluation of personal selling efforts remains not only important but actually crucial even in an era of direct marketing through mail, television and on-line services. The process of providing a product/service to the ultimate user requires a dedicated network of people who must sincerely believe in the price/value/quality/performance of whatever is being sold. Personal selling involves not only salespeople, brokers, agents, etc. It must involve customer assistance—handling telephone conversations, inquiries and complaints at all levels and phases of the distribution process, from raw materials to the finished product or service purchased by the ultimate user.

b. Promotion—Many companies still believe that the customer, particularly the consumer, is ignorant, stupid, misinformed and gullible. Their promotion and advertising are geared to deceive. Every consumer may not be a space scientist, but consumers are becoming smarter than the advertising agencies' target prototype. Many enterprises are learning an important lesson at great expense: *don't promise what you can't deliver!* Japanese automaker Mitsubishi initiated in September 1994 a broad and very expensive full-page color magazine advertising campaign for its new luxury $60,000 sports car named Spyder. The first model wasn't available for viewing and sale at a large dealership in Florida until July 1, 1995—ten months later!

c. Place—Marketing is still an art and a practice, not an exact science. It requires continuous assessment of many variables and a subjective judgment as to the best action to take. A key decision relates to the place of physical or virtual (e.g., on-line computer network or television screen) purchasing access for the potential customer of your product/service. That special place determines the logistics of delivery, distribution, production and all the many functions required for proper servicing of the place where the customer buys.

d. New Technologies—The proliferation and growth of electronic communication opens new horizons for extending markets and reaching present and new customers. Direct marketing is now easier because of ready availability of consumers' phone numbers and addresses on inexpensive CDs. Marketing through cable television (e.g., infomercials) is reaching new levels of sophistication and revulsion. Customers can be reached by phone, fax, cable and satellite in addition to mail and printed media. The advent of interactive communication will further enhance and complicate the delivery of the sellers' messages. As customers are increasingly bombarded with sales pitches from all directions, they are also becoming more sophisticated, educated and skeptical. Don't underestimate the power and the new attitudes of the ultimate consumer.

Knowledge is of two kinds. We know the subject ourselves,
or we know where to find information upon it.

Samuel Johnson (1775)

HOLE 10   MARKETING   PAR 5

SCORING

	Stroke Description	Hazard Description	BAD Double Bogey +2	SO/SO Bogey +1	GOOD Par 0	SUPER Birdie −1
1	We continuously monitor the market's pulse to rapidly adjust our product/service to new demands.	a) Inside-out myopia. b) Overemphasizing the role of technology vs. the *soft touch.*				
2	We continuously ask all our markets: *Where and how is it the easiest for the customer to do business with us?*	Conducting business in ways that are convenient for the company. Selfish interest prevails.				
3	We base our product and service decisions on the inputs from the marketplace from customers, prospects and the public.	a) We know better what the customer wants! b) Engineers dominate the marketeers. CEO's hunches are infallible!				
4	We price to the market. We consider the economic value of the product/service to the customer.	a) We price according to our costs. b) We modify our products/services to meet cost/profit ratios.				
5	We practice personal selling, honest promotion and proper sales places to genuinely benefit our customers. True service, no *hype*!	a) Wasting money in promotion of new items not ready for market. b) Exaggerated claims. c) Selling places convenient to us.				

HOLE 10   MARKETING   PAR 5

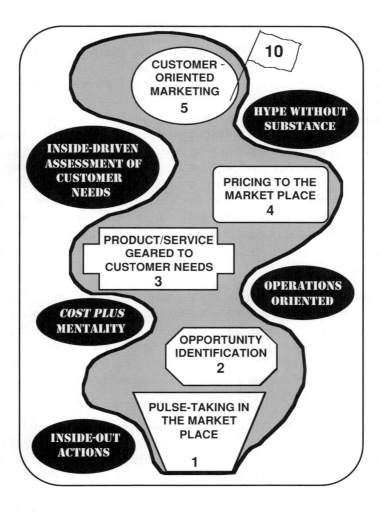

Business has only two basic functions: marketing and innovation.

Peter Drucker (1962)

HOLE 11   PRODUCTION   PAR 4

PRO'S COMMENTS

1. PRODUCTION SOURCE—Production, supply and subcontract sources are no longer limited to national or geographical constraints. The world is pretty much an open arena, and the key word is *global*. The multiplicity of selection is rising to a complex combination of multinational production, subcontracting, alliances, partnerships, outright purchases, barter and just-in-time deliveries. Even such a simple staple as apple juice is produced in the United States from imported concentrates manufactured in Argentina, Austria, Germany, Hungary and Italy. The size of a company does not preclude global transactions and procurement. It does require greater knowledge and a new *worldly* outlook by owners and management. Larger enterprises must become more sophisticated in their evaluation of large capital investments vs. future political, economic and social changes in the countries of their partners.

2. LOCATION—While there are many production sources, in existence or potential, an important policy decision must be made as to the actual geography of production. Here, again, the criteria and choices are many and increasing each year. A sound strategy must be developed for a set of priorities for production site selection. Which comes first: proximity of market, cost of production, regional stability, barter opportunities or future potential?

3. FLEXIBILITY—Because world conditions change so rapidly and unpredictably (e.g., the crash of the Mexican peso and major losses of foreign investments in early 1995), flexibility—the ability to change and adjust rapidly to any event—has become priority one in the key decision making and strategies of enterprises. Flexibility means the competence for complete reversal of previous decisions, including hard investments in plant and equipment, without suffering catastrophic losses. We have to learn to hedge against unpredictability and insure ourselves, even at a relatively high cost, against our growing inability to forecast the future.

4. SHORTER CYCLE TIME—We are witnessing an overall acceleration of human-controlled events throughout the world. Technological breakthroughs occur faster and faster. Consumers' likes and dislikes change faster. There are shorter economic cycles. Even politicians last less time in power. The phenomenon of compression of time is extremely important in running a business which must respond to the outside-in pressures of the external environment. Thus, R&D projects must be completed faster, production runs must be faster, inventories must be smaller and just-in-time, deliveries must be faster, and delays must be eliminated or greatly reduced. The process can be described as the urgent need to shorten the *throughput time* from the original order to delivery to the ultimate user. Successful companies have been doing it and continue to work on shortening the time span of all phases of their operations.

Production is not application of tools to materials,
but logic to work!

Peter Drucker (1973)

HOLE 11   PRODUCTION   PAR 4

SCORING

	Stroke Description	Hazard Description	BAD Double Bogey +2	SO/SO Bogey +1	GOOD Par 0	SUPER Birdie −1
1	We recognize and practice the new need for expanding our production capacity beyond our own walls.	a) Insufficient *due* diligence in acquiring allies or partners. b) Insufficient long-term look into future production needs and criteria.				
2	We have thoroughly analyzed our location needs. We have clearly identified present and future priorities.	Provincial attitude of liking everything to be similar or close to *home.*				
3	We recognize and practice flexibility as one of the most important needs and most powerful tools in a competitive battle.	Making long-term production decisions which may lock the company into long-term shackles.				
4	All our business processes are continuously reworked to speed up the throughput cycle.	Considering cycle time as an internal characteristic, instead of major customer demand and high external priority.				

HOLE 11   **PRODUCTION**   **PAR 4**

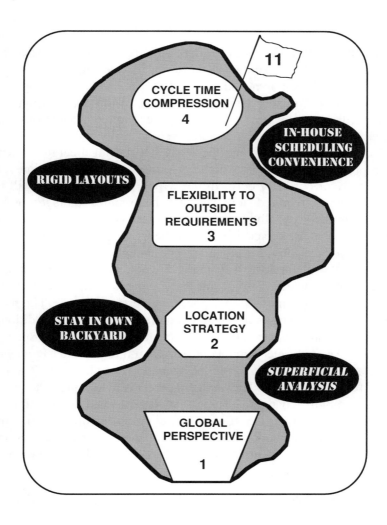

PRO'S COMMENTS

1. KINDS OF WORK—The work of any organization is carried out with a variety of occupations. Occupations require people's skills and physical tools, such as machines, facilities, methods and integration of workflows. To understand how the work of the organization will be carried out, it is necessary to classify the required occupations with a clear definition of the kinds and levels of skills and tools needed. These specifications become the basis for staffing operations with appropriate people and nonhuman resources. If the occupations are not clearly or correctly defined, the wrong persons or tools will be selected for the required slots. Whether the organization is *flat* or *fat*, it is still necessary to divide the work to make certain it all gets done. All functions must be specified, from the CEO to the janitorial function. Obviously, job titles alone are not enough.

It's not a platitude to say that all work, in any endeavor and throughout the world, has become more complicated, more sophisticated and requires more knowledge to be performed well. The most menial and simple tasks may today require new skills and additional training, because of the introduction of automated devices, such as scanners, keypads, electronic controls, monitors and other *efficiency* devices. The demand for unskilled workers is diminishing. The demand for specialists and knowledge workers is increasing. The workplace is rapidly changing. There's an urgent need for continuous reevaluation of tasks, workflows, processes and people's skills and specifications. The work revolution is a challenge for employers and a hard new reality for employees. It will need a readjustment on both ends of the spectrum.

2. CORE COMPETENCIES—The day-to-day tasks and activities of any organization are carried out through functions that are pretty much generic to all organizations, such as selling, purchasing, producing, administering, training and accounting. It is important to distinguish between generic functions that apply to all organizations and the specific needs and procedures for your business and your organization. Defining the essential, specific and pertinent core competencies for your business is a very important, if not crucial, task for top management. These range from deep knowledge of certain technologies to production processes to information systems to distribution logistics to marketing, selling and service techniques. These competencies must be kept up to date to maintain one's superiority in a field or a niche. Global benchmarking of specific functions is a useful and constructive means of auditing one's alertness and progress. It should be done objectively and addressed with a self-critical attitude. Because of fast change and rapid obsolescence, continuous improvement of one's core competencies is also a must. No organization has the means to be the best in everything it does. Proper selection of core competencies and concentration on what really matters are essential ingredients of success.

3. INNOVATIONS—Doing the same work in the same old way belies the whole concept of change and progress. If change is occurring, then the work to be done must also change. If not, the work will become outdated, outmoded and inefficient.

A philosophy of innovation for continuous improvement was, in the past, a part of the R&D effort, but R&D was too limited in that it related mostly to product technology and product improvement. Today, every task, procedure, business process, service, system, information flow and, of course, product must be looked at from an innovative viewpoint. Value engineering was one of the forerunners of the concept of providing value-added products and services to the customer, for which money was received by the company. Today, innovative efforts must span all operations within an organization, aiming at additional revenues, lower costs and greater efficiency and speed of results. Innovation effort cannot be limited to any function or department. It must encompass every facet of an organization and requires everyone's participation.

Because of the scarcity of funds that exists at any level of any organization, a precise allocation of precious and discretionary R&D

and innovation monies is important and difficult. A lot of clever thought and analysis must be applied to the decision on what projects to fund. It's a risk call, most often a gamble. Management must decide where to put the chips and how long to keep feeding the kitty. The best advice is not to spread the risk over many projects. They'll end up underfunded and overdue. It's better to select a few targets and go for them. Periodic and objective analysis of progress is obviously essential.

4. CONTINUOUS UPGRADING—Continuous acquisition and use of new techniques is essential for the viability of any enterprise. Core competencies change faster as technology progresses faster. They also can become obsolete when previously nonrelated fields converge and often drastically change the status quo; for example, breakthroughs in electronic imaging (chips and digital technology) affect the photographic film industry by potentially making silver halide chemistry obsolete. Redesigning work is not a luxury; it's a necessity. It has to be done well, professionally and continuously. It requires proper budgets and a great deal of attention and know-how. The function will grow in need, costs and complexity as the technological revolution impacts all phases of human endeavor, faster and deeper.

Proper selection of skills, tools, materials and methods, as well as optimum delivery, better and faster results in performance and retention, require dedicated professionals/specialists inside and outside the company. The review of the entire work development program and process is the responsibility of the highest level of management—the board of directors and the CEO. The future of the business depends on it.

If you have great talents, industry will improve them. If you have but moderate abilities, industry will supply their deficiency.

Sir Joshua Reynolds (1769)

HOLE 12   WORK   PAR 4

SCORING

	Stroke Description	Hazard Description	BAD Double Bogey +2	SO/SO Bogey +1	GOOD Par 0	SUPER Birdie −1
1	Our skill classification is complete, up to date and *alive*. All jobs have been identified and described.	a) Skill classification and job descriptions are not considered a priority need. b) *It's better to wing it!*				
2	We clearly understand and define our core competencies. We match our skills to support them.	a) Missing subtle changes in required core competencies. b) Missing breakthrough in non-competing area which will change our core competency definition.				
3	We support innovation and continuous improvement at all levels. We encourage it. We reward it.	a) We talk innovation and support status quo. b) Innovative ideas are not implemented.				
4	We continually train our employees with latest and best techniques to keep our core competencies at the highest level.	Perfunctory training, not given very high priority or attention. Lack of continuity because of budget cuts and fluctuations.				

HOLE 12   **WORK**   PAR 4

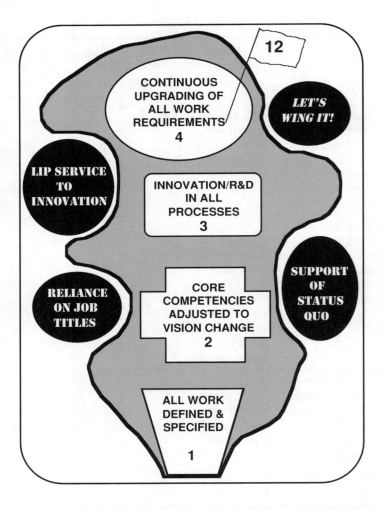

It takes little talent to see clearly what lies under one's nose, a good deal of it to know in which direction to point that organ.

W. H. Auden, poet (1962)

HOLE 13   PEOPLE   PAR 4

PRO'S COMMENTS

1. HUMAN RESOURCE—In the past and with industrialization, people were considered the *labor component*. They were a *thing,* like capital and machinery. This perception has changed very slowly and very gradually. During the past decades, businesses began treating some people as human beings. Recent massive layoffs, throughout the industrial world, but mainly in the United States, show that there is still a long way to go. The acceptance by business of the inherent difference between *humans* and *things* is not yet a universally practiced policy. Obviously, the difference is that people have an intelligence that allows them to make improvements and breakthroughs in the way things work. All such advancements are the result of human application. By tapping into people's intelligence potential, the skills, work and results of an organization can be greatly enhanced.

Talented, well-trained, highly motivated employees are the greatest asset of any organization. They don't want to stand still and do the same job all their lives. The United States was known and envied for the great upward mobility of its labor force. When a company grew and prospered, many opportunities were opened for promotion and new jobs. New times have seriously impaired the scope and the frequency of upward promotions. Global competitive pressures, mergers, alliances, subcontracting, consolidations and, above all, technology have reduced the employment needed at any level for the proper function of any business. The new reality is that we need fewer people to maintain excellent performance of a business. This trend will continue, and promotion opportunities will become even rarer in the future. It's very important for all employees to understand the changing conditions and how their lives and careers will be affected. Many companies substitute for upward opportunity with lateral opportunity. Rotation of personnel through various departments and various disciplines broadens individuals. They become knowledgeable in a variety of subjects and can perform many different jobs. There is increasing demand for multidisciplinary talent. New opportunities are open for geographical transfers, nationally and internationally. The very ambitious and the very impatient should seek their fortunes by becoming entrepreneurs and starting their own companies, where the opportunities are still unlimited, although risky.

Operating in today's environment requires two classifications of people for purposes of work: *core occupation* workers and *knowledge* workers.

2. CORE OCCUPATIONS—The era of knowledge and technology requires a higher skill level of all employees at any job throughout any organization. It's an established and accepted fact that the success of an enterprise depends on its proficiency in its *core competencies.* These must be carried out through skillful people, working with the best tools. The required capabilities must be understood, analyzed, classified, evaluated and continuously upgraded and improved. This is the only way to stay ahead of the competition and in tune with new technological developments. The skills of employees are a crucial resource of an organization. They must be matched to the competencies required to carry on the business of the company. The results expected in any function must be based on the best linking of the individual to the high requirements/expectations of performance.

In addition to a precise determination of key core competencies, we need a precise inventory of individual skills to establish the degree of present proficiency and the necessary criteria for continuous improvement. This is not a peripheral assignment to a staff in personnel relations. This is a key line function to assure survival, progress and a valid competitive advantage.

3. KNOWLEDGE WORKERS—The industrial world successively evolved from 5,000 years of agriculture to 300 years of industrial production to 60 years of a service economy to the last 15 years of primacy of knowledge. The dominant force of change in all human endeavors is technology. It produces an ever-faster and deeper impact on human civilization because of the dramatically shorter intervals between major scientific breakthroughs. The explosion of new knowledge and the resulting new conditions in all phases of business operations are produced by talented, knowledgeable, creative, imaginative people. They are absolutely essential for success or even just the survival of any human organization.

Every business must take a thorough and honest inventory of its most talented individuals in all its areas of endeavor: marketing, production, development, systems, general management. They are and will be the *knowledge drivers* of the organization and its future. They are not necessarily the top managers. The most important characteristic of a good CEO is his/her ability to recognize, attract and keep talented people! You don't need many to make a major difference, but you absolutely need them. The authors call them *gorillas*. They make the difference between mediocrity and success, between failure and progress. Find them, inventory them and analyze your situation. Do you have any? Do you have enough? Are they real gorillas or monkeys in disguise? If you don't have enough, why not? What are the real reasons? Analyze, dissect, learn and act. The future of your enterprise depends on it!

Knowledge and information must be clearly differentiated in management's policies to keep upgrading the level of aptitude of the employees. A serious program of lifelong continuous learning to keep up with knowledge explosion must be instituted for all key managers and highly talented employees. These are the people who will make a difference! The *chosen* must make a personal commitment to diligently pursue a custom-tailored program of continual improvement of their education, knowledge and understanding of the world around them. The program is essential to prevent personal and professional obsolescence, which can occur within four years or less. The commitment requires around seven to ten hours a week devoted to customized self-improvement.

Talented people require a free and multifaceted environment that encourages creativity and self-expression. It's an environment of give-and-take, unfettered exchange of views, constructive criticism, continuous challenge and nonpunitive opposition. It's a place where people thrive on new ideas, on freedom to experiment and on acceptance of some degree of failure. Not all new concepts will succeed. A policy of "one error and you're out" is not conducive to innovation. The environment of intellectual freedom and self-expression is neither idealistic nor theoretical. It includes challenges, constructive conflict, intellectual battles, many disagreements and a degree of tension and pressure. The overall blend is, however, positive and results-oriented.

4. REWARDS AND MOTIVATIONS—In addition to the free-wheeling company environment, a progressive company must institute reward programs, aimed directly at stimulating and enhancing creativity and innovation. Broad incentive programs don't appeal to *gorillas*. The most effective way to reward an unusual individual or a small creative team is the *cafeteria-style rewards menu*. Ask the person what he/she wants! It may be a salary increase, a stock option, a large bonus, an extended vacation, a reduced work schedule or a red Ferrari. *Whatever a gorilla wants, a gorilla gets* should be the policy, despite the protestations of the human resources department. Don't listen to bureaucrats and paper pushers. They'll always claim that individually tailored rewards will create administrative nightmares and morale problems. Don't standardize, personalize. Do what works, not what's convenient.

Everyone needs encouragement and some reward beyond the regular paycheck. Most employees want to do a good job, but they also want their efforts recognized and acknowledged. It's impractical to establish a personal, customized reward and motivation program for every single employee, similar to the *what do you want?* process for the company's *gorillas*. But there's a lot that can be done—much more than most companies are doing in times of budget cutting and layoffs. Employees need a lot of positive reinforcement and a feeling of belonging and being wanted in today's times of uncertainty and layoffs. Written policies and letters from the president are not credible. Personal, face-to-face communications are most effective, if they are sincere. Rewards must be individual or small-group oriented. Overall rewards based on total company or even division performance are ineffective because the individual has no control over the results.

Suggestion programs can be very valuable to the company and the employee if they are administered correctly. Suggestions must be judged fairly and rapidly. Proper reply and explanation must be given to each submitter promptly. The amount of reward must be meaningful. If the suggestion produces verified annual savings of $1 million, the originator should receive 50 percent of the savings or $500,000! That creates attention and incentive for many other valuable suggestions.

The person with a new idea is a crank until the idea succeeds.

Mark Twain (1897)

HOLE 13   PEOPLE   PAR 4

SCORING

	Stroke Description	Hazard Description	BAD Double Bogey +2	SO/SO Bogey +1	GOOD Par 0	SUPER Birdie −1
1	We respect all our employees as our greatest asset. We treat them accordingly.	a) Most of our employees are a disposable *labor component*. b) We can't afford a *soft touch* approach.				
2	We carefully match our core competencies to the skills of our employees. We keep the process current and dynamic.	The work force is too unstable and unreliable to invest a lot of training dollars in upgrading skills.				
3	We actively maintain a talent inventory and support the *gorilla* concept. Innovation and creativity are our number one priority.	a) Our motto is: *No one is indispensable.* b) We don't support *prima donnas.*				
4	Our individual super-reward program recognizes individual and team performance in unique ways.	a) We treat all employees equally. b) Special rewards are expensive and unfair.				

HOLE 13   PEOPLE   PAR 4

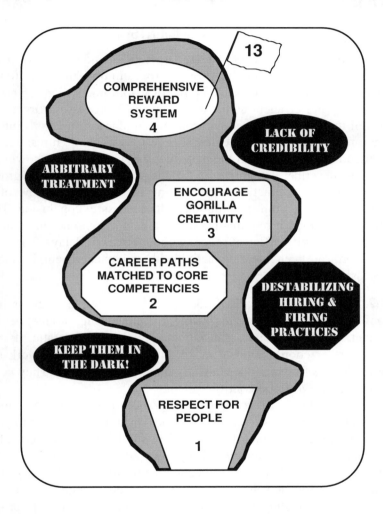

Leadership is the art of
getting superior performance from ordinary people.

John D. Rockefeller (1905)

HOLE 14   *SYSTEMS*   PAR 3

PRO'S COMMENTS

1. WORKFLOWS—Computerized operations and electronic communications depend on the proper programming of data flows, from input to output. The same is true of *workflows,* which represent an orderly and efficient **sequence** of business processes. Organizations of the past were based on grouping similar job functions into a department, each a separate entity. The result was static. It resulted in the pseudo-optimization of the parts, not the whole. It was, however, easier to describe, categorize and manage. Today, we must group together different functions contributing to the efficient flow of a business process, from its initiation to its successful conclusion. The effect is dynamic; it requires passing the baton from one function to another, in a swift, efficient mode, without errors or delays. The new catchwords are reengineering, activities-based management, business process analysis, etc.

2. INTEGRATION OF PROCESSES—Even a simple business has many different workflows: marketing, manufacturing, product development, etc. Even if its organization is dynamic, not static, it still needs further coordination to make all functions properly work together. Rivers flowing independently may cause flooding. They need a comprehensive flood control system.

The main factor for successful integration of processes is human teamwork. Managers of various functions must work together to produce an efficient and interdependent flow of all processes needed for the operation of an enterprise. They must talk to each other, understand each other's functions and cooperate for the overall good of the business, not for the sole efficiency of their departments. This is not a *motherhood* statement. It's a key requirement of greatest priority.

3. POSITIVE CHANGE—Continuous change requires continuous adaptation and continuous improvement. The area of systems and processes is the heart of the organization, pumping vital blood to all its parts. It has to be viewed as an evolving, interdependent organism. It requires attention to details and ongoing innovative improvement of all its various functions and facets. But it also needs constant attention to the overall results. That's why management must watch, coordinate and encourage teams to work together, aiming at improvement of the whole. The need for interdisciplinary knowledge is again evident and must be encouraged.

Benchmarking is a useful method to judge the scope and speed of positive change. Establish a system for comparison of every important function in your company against the performance of the same function by a global leader in the field. It doesn't necessarily have to be a competitor. Compare yourself to the best practices, anywhere in the world, in personnel motivation, robotics, computer systems, research methods, marketing promotion, etc. Don't compare yourself to entire companies but rather to individual functions in various organizations.

If you can't explain it simply, you don't understand it well enough.

Albert Einstein (1947)

HOLE 14   SYSTEMS   PAR 3

SCORING

	Stroke Description	Hazard Description	BAD Double Bogey +2	SO/SO Bogey +1	GOOD Par 0	SUPER Birdie −1
1	We are organized by workflows to achieve greater efficiency. All workflows are directed from outside-in for the benefit of the customer.	a) We talk work-flows but are controlled by departments. b) Our people don't have the multidisciplinary workflow knowledge They're single-function specialists.				
2	We are good at coordinating and optimizing the workflows and the working re-lationships among all individuals, departments and functions of the organization.	a) Our managers protect their re-spective turfs and feifdoms. b) Our organiza-tion is not geared to *flows* of activities.				
3	We diligently pursue a program of continuous improvement in all our workflows (systems and processes).	a) Improvement efforts are still compartmentalized by functions and departments. b) Lack of overall, supra-depart-mental continuous improvement effort.				

HOLE 14   SYSTEMS   PAR 3

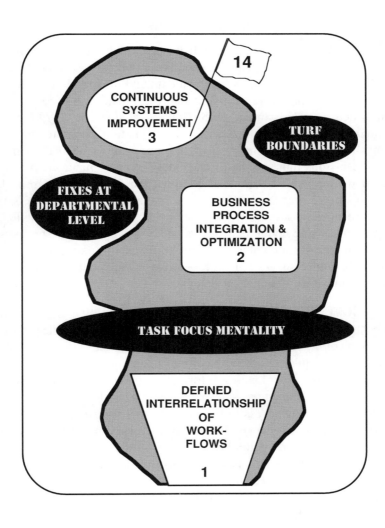

HOLE 15 INFORMATION PAR 4

PRO'S COMMENTS

1. DATABASES—Since the advent of the computer, there is seldom a shortage of data. There's usually an overflow, a flood of data. It's important to distinguish between data and information. Although it's evident, a common mistake of many companies is to rely on the data-processing department, MIS, EDP or whatever it may be called to analyze and supply the operating information needs to management. That's wrong! The task of defining what's needed to make better decisions must be the primary duty of each manager. An individual who doesn't know what combination of data is essential for best job performance should not be managing. Information is the driving force for success in any enterprise. Obviously, a knowledge worker and a knowledge manager must know what data are necessary to be transformed into valuable information and ultimately into knowledge. The entire success of an enterprise is dependent on that flow. That responsibility cannot be delegated.

2. COMPUTER NETWORKS—Network technology is improving daily and rapidly. Remote access to databases is now possible throughout the world, in the office, at home and on the road. The latest advances will link laptops with cellular telephones and satellite communications for downloading information under any conditions and circumstances. Managers, salespeople and knowledge workers will have instantaneous access to the most current information needed to improve their performance. There's an increasing need to revise and redesign one's work patterns to take the fullest advantage of data network capabilities. This new dimension adds many new opportunities to businesses everywhere. It transcends barriers of geography, time and travel. It requires a new mindset and new technical and psychological adaptation to a new way of work patterns.

Electronic communication is a tool and only a tool. It's a grave mistake to use electronics as a substitute for human interchange, empathy and understanding. A good modern manager understands how to blend the *hard* and the *soft* touch.

3. *LIVING* SYSTEMS—The flow and transformation of data into information and ultimately into knowledge can be compared to a *living* organism that requires a timely peripheral input of nutrients to be transformed into the healthy growth of the whole organism. It also requires periodic elimination of waste to avoid contamination and decay. It parallels the needs of an organization for the continuous and timely input of data reflecting all its external and internal operations or transactions. These data must be cleverly and efficiently transformed into valid and valuable information to nourish managers and knowledge workers for better/faster decisions and actions for continuous improvement of the enterprise. It's also essential to constantly examine the data input to check on the adequacy, correctness and usefulness of the data and information it generates. Old, obsolete or useless data must be discarded to prevent data clutter, information overflow and obfuscation of what's really important. This *firm grasp of the obvious* is not always followed. There are too many examples of system failures, inadequacies and confusion.

There's a need for further *transformation* of top management's attitude toward data and information. Timely information and the latest knowledge are not addenda to the management process; they're the key and the driving force of the enterprise. A *living system* of information flow cannot be delegated to a department or a computer center. It must become the prime focus of every individual in the organization. It must be universally understood and practiced that information is the *life blood* of the enterprise. It must continuously circulate and regenerate, healthy, clean and uncontaminated.

4. COMPUTER LITERACY—There's no excuse, in today's environment, for tolerating computer illiterates at any level of the organization. Yet, it's a common problem. There are CEOs who *hate* computers. They are psychologically turned off, despite their acknowledgment of the need for the electronic *gadgets*! Top management's attitudes cannot be hidden and will have an adverse effect on the whole organization. The opposite problem arises with computer *addicts* who neglect vital personal contacts and exchange of living ideas by hiding behind the impersonal protective curtain of a computer monitor. Computerized retailing, distribution, production processes, point-of-sale recorders and even taxicab dispatch devices require some computer-use knowledge from grass-roots workers and the lowest paid employees. Experience has shown that American workers display one of the highest functional illiteracy rates in the industrial world. Some 30 million American workers, presently employed, cannot properly read or perform the simplest arithmetic function! Obviously, remedial measures—teaching the 3Rs—should be taken before such a handicapped individual can be asked to generate and start using information on a computer.

Information networks straddle the world. Nothing remains concealed. But the sheer volume of information dissolves the information. We are unable to take it all in.

Günther Grass (1990)

Knowledge in the form of international commodity indispensable to productive power is already, and will continue to be, a major—perhaps the major—stake in worldwide competition for power. It is conceivable that nation-states will one day fight for control of information, just as they battled in the past for control over territory.

Jean François Lyotard, philosopher (1979)

HOLE 15   INFORMATION   PAR 4

SCORING

Stroke Description	Hazard Description	BAD Double Bogey +2	SO/SO Bogey +1	GOOD Par 0	SUPER Birdie −1
1 Our databases have been designed by users, who continuously supply input to update and upgrade the system.	a) Databases are designed by the computer experts. b) Excessive clutter of non-essential data.				
2 We have in place efficient, practical electronic networks. They're fully used by all whose jobs are improved by on-line communications.	a) Network clutter and abuse by those without *need to know.* b) Substituting technology for essential human face-to-face rapport.				
3 Our computer and network systems are truly up to date. We can rely on the currency of information.	a) Currency of data is a major question. b) Information formats are too rigid—not changing with change.				
4 All our personnel are computer literate. They know how to use latest technology and like to do it.	a) We have computer illiterates among our top management. b) Computer literacy is not our major priority.				

HOLE 15   INFORMATION   PAR 4

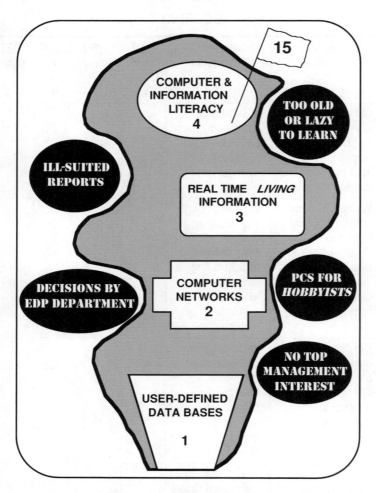

To know that we know what we know, and that
we do not know what we do not know: that is true knowledge.

Confucius (460 B.C.)

HOLE 16 RESESOURCES PAR 5

PRO'S COMMENTS

1. VIABILITY—It's sometimes tough to face the reality that most physical resources of a business are obsolete or very obsolescent. Today's rapidly changing environment and even faster changing technology make it almost impossible to keep all one's physical resources up to date. Many companies may have invested large sums in corporate headquarters. Today's concept of decentralization, combined with electronic communications, make corporate headquarters resemble mummified dinosaurs. Companies are paring their corporate staffs from thousands to a few dozen. Even preferred locations are changing from large metropolitan centers to small, rural, relatively safer, remote hinterlands.

Factories have purchased, tried and discarded expensive robots. Mainframe computers are being replaced by servers and computer networks. This may require programming changes at a cost of millions and millions of dollars. Distribution centers are either being consolidated (fewer but larger) or eliminated (direct deliveries from manufacturers to retail outlets). Branch offices are being closed. Sales and service personnel can operate out of their homes and cars, yet be in continuous contact with dispatch and computer databases.

It's very important to analyze thoroughly and objectively all capital investment items and decide on their present usefulness and degree of obsolescence. The analysis should be creative. Don't think physical replacement; think *function* replacement. It may be something totally different. The key objective is to achieve the same or better results without physical facilities and capital investment.

2. TOOLS—Children in today's grade schools learn about the progression of human beings from stone-carved tool users to computer-driven robot controllers. The concept of any tool, from the simplest to the most complex, is to improve human productivity. We want to leverage human output to a higher level for an economic price. Whatever we do or buy must respond positively to the above equation. Managers must analyze *every* function in the business to determine what kind of financial physical investment per employee will improve performance and profitability. Some minor investment may provide very high returns. On the other hand, billions of dollars invested during the eighties in complex robots for automobile assembly lines were scrapped a few years later. You should never try to improve a part (single station) of a workflow without a thorough understanding of the effect on the entire process. Major production and productivity improvements at one or even several stations may backfire by producing bottlenecks, waiting lines and chaos on the line as a whole.

3. AUTOMATION—The ultimate tool is the complete automation of a process and elimination of all operators. The effects of such major automation usually receive negative publicity because they result in elimination of jobs, layoffs and unemployment. Actually, total automation reduces and changes employment characteristics. It never eliminates all jobs, but that explanation is of small consolation to the bank teller displaced by the ATM machine. On the other hand, ATM producers increase their R&D staff, production line operators and maintenance and service staff. The overall trend in *total automation* transformation is a net decrease in total employment. This is the first time in history that automation technology is contributing to a net decrease in overall employment. In the past, after an initial dislocation and shift from agriculture to manufacturing to services, technology was a positive force in providing new jobs. The structural negative shift started in the middle eighties and will continue into the twenty-first century.

Management of a competitive enterprise must consider all means of reducing costs and improving productivity and performance, without consideration of economic effects on the society as a whole. It is a socially unfortunate situation, but a given in a free-enterprise, capitalistic society. If you don't do it, competitors will. It is better to reduce one's employment by 10 percent than to become noncompetitive, go out of business and lay off 100 percent.

4. VALUE TO THE CUSTOMER—It was mentioned several times before that *outside-in* thinking and practice must prevail in all phases of a company's operations. The repetition is intentional, because of the importance of the concept. Often in the past, decisions on capital investment and physical resources dealt primarily with return on investment and effects on the P&L. Today, the first question and consideration must be: *How will this investment improve the value of our product/service to our customer or bring in new customers?* Obviously, the financial considerations are very important, but they must come second. Paradoxically, if the financial considerations are positive but there is no immediate tangible added value to the customer, management may want to think twice before allocating funds. Promise and lure of increased profits, without additional customer value, may be a short-term trap or just an illusion.

5. OUTSOURCING—Strategies of extensive vertical and horizontal integration within the boundaries of a single corporation were abandoned a long time ago. Automotive manufacturers no longer own iron mines and foundries to produce their own brake housings and transmission covers. Today, there is a global overabundance of technologies, raw materials and physical and intellectual resources to supplement and service the needs of any business, anywhere. The outsourcing can be done in many ways: subcontractor, partnership, joint venture, alliance, etc. A progressive company must have thorough knowledge of all the possibilities and offerings, worldwide. The data must be fresh, and high-quality analysis should be updated at short intervals. Outsourcing is no longer a specialized function delegated to the purchasing department. It's a major strategic consideration that requires top management policies, key decisions and dedicated follow-up. It's another example of major changes in priorities and philosophies of running an organization in today's new times.

Don't plan vast projects with half-vast resources!

Anon.

HOLE 16   **RESOURCES**   PAR 5

SCORING

	Stroke Description	Hazard Description	BAD Double Bogey +2	SO/SO Bogey +1	GOOD Par 0	SUPER Birdie −1
1	We continuously analyze our physical resources to determine their operational viability and systematic replacement.	a) *We have it, we'll stick with it* policy. b) Postponing important system and organization changes because of physical constraints.				
2	All managers are charged with responsibility to analyze and propose new *tools* for improved overall performance.	Excessive dependence on recommendations from departmental people, subject to potential *myopia*.				
3	Our management teams pay special attention to total automation concepts, even if it changes the structure of the whole business.	a) We are weary of drastic changes in our physical processes. b) We are locked in because of inflexible processes of the past.				
4	Value to the customer is always our first consideration and priority in any discussion or proposal.	Investment in physical assets is dictated by financial criteria of ROI and P&L.				
5	We consider outsourcing as an equal partner of in-house production and productivity.	a) More *comfortable* with in-house operations. b) Fear of competitive disclosure and vulnerability.				

HOLE 16   RESOURCES   PAR 5

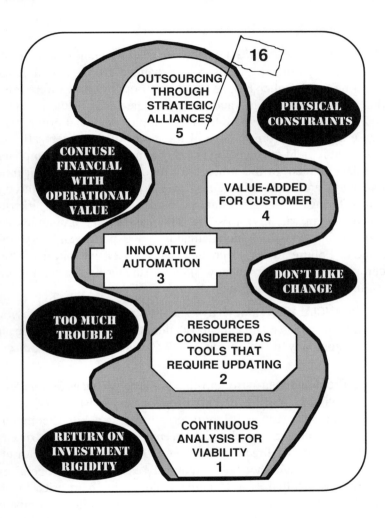

There's a better way to do it. Find it!

Thomas A. Edison (1880)

PRO'S COMMENTS

1. FINANCING/FUNDING—Finance used to be a fancy name for the accounting department. As its role expanded from general ledger accounting to controllership, new and better opportunities were found and devised for employing and deploying the funds of the organization. This led to a whole new field of complex financial programs to increase the return from the use of the assets of the organization.

The whole field of financing is today a major strategic component in the development of the strategy for a corporation. Different innovative ways are constantly being devised to better finance through public offerings, strategic alliances, banking relationships, international routes, private investors, etc. This has become a complex and highly specialized field, which demands high expertise and very good judgment. Failure to do so creates many expensive pitfalls which occur at an increasing frequency and with staggering financial results (e.g., investments and speculation in derivatives).

2. FINANCIAL STATEMENTS—The two traditional and obvious areas of focus which receive the most attention and scrutiny inside and outside a company are the *profit-and-loss statement* and the *balance sheet.*

    a. Profit-and-loss—Bottom-line thinking produces *bottom feeders.* Obviously profit is essential for the very existence of a business, but obsession with short-term profit can kill a company, rather than save it. American *quartermania* is a contagious disease with the board of directors and the CEO as primary virus carriers. Recently, a small shortfall in quarterly earnings vs. brokers' expectations resulted in a 35 percent plunge in share price in one day! The company was Sensormatic, a solid, well-run company, with excellent growth and performance potential. In a global environment, with global competition, the U.S. preoccupation with quarter-to-quarter/dollars-per-share results often induces long-term nightmares. Neither Japanese nor European companies had as short an outlook as U.S. public companies. Thus, they could make long-term moves and implement their strategies more consistently than their American counterparts. The trend is changing. The short-term thinking is contaminating public companies worldwide.

b. Balance Sheet—A company's foundation is the balance sheet. It's the base upon which a company grows and prospers. It must be solid, real and honest. It should reflect the company's genuine position for strategic decisions about the future. Recently, respectable companies made major errors by allowing their financial officers to operate the finance department as a profit center! In many cases, this led to excesses: betting, not hedging, on derivatives, on foreign exchange and on future oil prices. Billions of dollars were lost unnecessarily by top executives who lost track of their fiduciary responsibilities and the definition of *what business they were in*! New conditions create new problems. High cash flow and accumulation of liquid assets are no longer healthy because they may stimulate hostile takeover bids. Some companies buy back their own stock. It's usually a stupid and desperate move, demonstrating to the public that top executives haven't a single constructive idea on how to invest stockholders' money in profitable production of goods and services!

3. RISK PHILOSOPHY—The initial entrepreneurial flair is usually a very high-risk affair. As a company grows, the risk factor begins to abate, except for special situations such as LBOs, hostile takeovers or speculative flurries. When a company begins to mature, risk is not described as philosophy but in terms of financial criteria. This is wrong. Every company needs a well-stated general philosophy of risk that supports the pursuit of corporate objectives. An unstated risk philosophy or one based only on financial ratios will hinder decisions on potential actions to pursue various growth opportunities. Selecting and funding opportunities is an ongoing and requisite responsibility of the top management team and the people who will be involved in the

---

Put not your trust in money, but put your money in trust.

Oliver Wendell Holmes (1858)

implementation of the growth strategies. Risk must be defined in terms of both financial exposure and *losses of opportunity*. Each company may have a different scale of risk strategies. Another *must* technique is calculating the cost of reversibility of a decision. What will be the total bill for reversing a risky decision after the full expenditure of required funds? If the cost of the reversal would force the company into bankruptcy, the original investment should not have been made. This technique places a practical limit on risk investments, according to a company's ability to weather adversity.

4. STAKEHOLDERS' SATISFACTION—The best way to express a public company's philosophy toward stakeholders is to quote from Harley-Davidson's annual report for 1995: *At Harley-Davidson, we don't run our business on a quarter-to-quarter basis. We also don't run our business for Wall Street, ourselves or even our customers. Our focus has been and will continue to be on long-term growth, which we believe is attainable only by balancing the interests of all our <u>stakeholders</u>. This way we all grow—together.* The stakeholders are customers, employees, suppliers, shareholders, financial institutions, the public and society. It would be desirable if many more public companies would embrace and practice Harley-Davidson's principles.

The key word is *practice*. Practically every public company publishes glowing statements about its noble intentions of satisfying stakeholders. Unfortunately, the number of cases of deceit, fraud and unethical behavior is increasing steadily. The most notorious violators of public trust are financial institutions or financial divisions of large conglomerates. Corporate CEOs should not be allowed to *delegate* blame to their subordinates or to plead ignorance. But they do!

The objects of a financier are to secure an ample revenue; to impose it with judgment and equality; to employ it economically; and, when necessity obliges him to make use of credit, to secure its foundations in that instance, and forever, by the clearness and candor of his proceedings, the exactness of his calculations, and the solidity of his funds.
                                                Edmund Burke (1790)

HOLE 17   FINANCE   PAR 4

SCORING

	Stroke Description	Hazard Description	BAD Double Bogey +2	SO/SO Bogey +1	GOOD Par 0	SUPER Birdie −1
1	We are knowledge-able in sophisticated worldwide financing. We are aware of all the angles and risks.	We have no in-ternal experts on financing. We rely on outsiders' advice and counsel!				
2	We do not run our company on a quarter-to-quarter basis. We do not run it for Wall Street. We run it for long-term growth and profitability. We have a properly valued balance sheet. We don't practice *imaginative* accounting.	a) Our real boss is a Wall Street *specialist* in our stock. b) Our balance sheet does not reflect our true value (obsolete inventories, under-funded pensions, overstated good-will).				
3	We have a clearly defined risk phil-osophy, defined at the top and under-stood by all managers.	a) Our limits of risk are unclear. b) We don't calculate the cost of reversibility of a risk decision.				
4	Our stakeholders are customers, employees, sup-pliers, shareholders, financial lenders, the public and society.	a) We run the business for the shareholders. b) We run the business for the enrichment of top management.				

HOLE 17   FINANCE   PAR 4

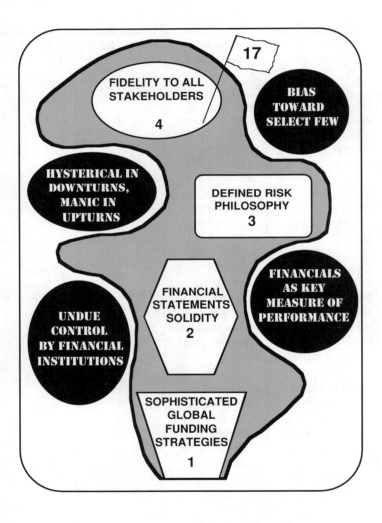

HOLE 18   PUBLIC RESPONSIBILITY   PAR 3

PRO'S COMMENTS

1. COMMUNITY—A company cannot exist in a vacuum. It needs each community where it operates as much as the community needs the business. There should be a mutually positive relationship. It's easier to achieve with smaller companies where the headquarters are located in the community and policy-making management is resident and participates in community affairs. A problem usually arises with long-distance, absentee management, unaware, uninterested and unconcerned with community relationships. This is a very shortsighted attitude. Without any altruistic reasons, a company should become an exemplary and proactive member of the community to extend its positive internal environment to the outside. It helps the local employees' morale, simplifies daily life and enhances the quality of *habitat.* A happy employee is a more productive employee. A happy community attracts talented people and reduces external distractions and hassles. It's a valuable asset, too often neglected or even seriously damaged by tunnel-vision, long-distance management.

2. NATIONAL—Businesses have a national responsibility to conduct their affairs legally, fairly and dependably. These should not be empty slogans. Draconian or *unfair* government regulations are brought about by corporate excesses, individually or industry-wide. These are costly to the businesses and to the people. Trade associations and large enterprises can be positive in self-policing, establishing voluntary fair standards of quality, safety, environmental protection and equal employment practices. They also can be self-serving, ruthless, corrupt and destructive. Any policy or action extended to the extreme will backfire and, in time, hurt the architects themselves. Unfortunately, the shortsightedness of many national and international giants and, sometimes, entire industries (e.g., tobacco, public construction, airlines) is appallingly stupid and counterproductive.

3. GLOBAL—Transnational operations are growing at an exponential rate. The planet is changing into a borderless marketplace.

Yet, it's also becoming increasingly pluralistic. The paradox creates major operating and policy dilemmas. How to achieve a unique operating blend of worldliness with provincialism? The challenge for any organization is to balance global policies with local adaptability. The problems and solutions are very, very difficult and ethically challenging. Do you move a highly polluting factory to a country with less rigid environmental regulations? Do you manufacture in regions with minimal wages, no benefits and no child labor restrictions? Do you practice bribery and condone corruption where they are accepted local customs? Is it possible for any organization to be successful worldwide with a uniform code of ethics and one standard of fairness and *good citizenship*? Each board of directors must consider these questions and act according to their collective conscience. But it is imperative that the matter of global ethics and behavior be brought up, debated and decided upon.

We are responsible for actions performed
in response to circumstances for which we are not responsible.

Allan Massie (1989)

HOLE 18   PUBLIC RESPONSIBILITY   PAR 3

SCORING

	Stroke Description	Hazard Description	BAD Double Bogey +2	SO/SO Bogey +1	GOOD Par 0	SUPER Birdie −1
1	We are proactive within every community where we do business. We are considered very good corporate citizens.	a) We don't get involved in community relations. b) We try to control the community for corporate advantage.				
2	We promote corporate and industry-wide practices in harmony with national needs and wants. Our policies don't conflict with social needs.	a) Our extensive lobbying aims to protect our interests and status quo. b) *What's good for our company is good for the country!*				
3	We have established, we practice and we enforce a uniform set of ethics in all our international operations.	Our ethics and policies are within the accepted *modus operandi* of each region.				

HOLE 18   PUBLIC RESPONSIBILITY   PAR 3

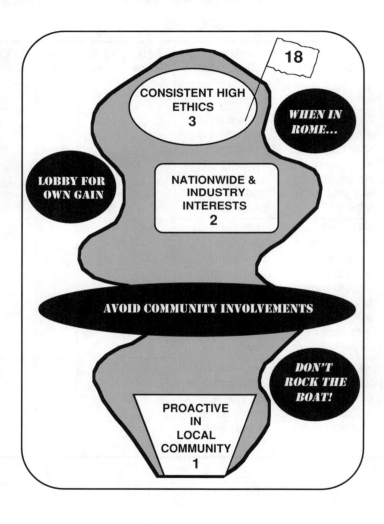

HOLE 19   HOW DID WE DO?

THE MOMENT OF TRUTH

SCORING TOTALS

Summarize your strokes vs. par for each of the 18 holes and write the numbers in the appropriate places in the table below. Add all the pars, birdies and bogeys to determine the overall score for your company. This score less 72 becomes your current handicap.

Hole	1	2	3	4	5	Score
1					■■■	
2					■■■	
3				■■■	■■■	
4						
5				■■■	■■■	
6					■■■	
7				■■■		
8						
9					■■■	
10						
11					■■■	
12					■■■	
13					■■■	
14				■■■	■■■	
15					■■■	
16						
17					■■■	
18				■■■	■■■	
PAR	■■■	■■■	■■■	■■■	■■■	

My company's score is:

95

If you rated your company's performance fairly and objectively, after reading the description of each stroke on every hole, you now have your first indication of your overall score in this highly competitive game of *management golf.*

This is just the beginning. Whatever your score is, there's room for improvement. First, analyze carefully all the holes where you scored above par. Your first step is to devise innovative action programs to improve the situation where it's most needed. The second step is to further enhance your already good performance, where you scored par, to a below-par excellence. Go to it!

Evaluation of Score and Handicap

Analysis of Individual Strokes

STEP ONE
Monday morning actions to remedy deficiencies
(above-par ratings)

1. _____
2. _____
3. _____
4. _____
5. _____

(add as many actions as necessary)

STEP TWO
Monday morning actions to capitalize on strengths
(par or below-par ratings)

1. _____
2. _____
3. _____
4. _____
5. _____

(add as many actions as necessary)

If you give people a fish, they will have a meal.
If you teach them to fish, they will have a living.
If you are thinking a year ahead, sow seed.
If you are thinking ten years ahead, plant a tree.
If you are thinking a hundred years ahead, educate the people.
By sowing seed once, you will harvest once.
By planting a tree, you will harvest tenfold.
By educating the people, you will harvest one hundredfold.

Anonymous Chinese poet (420 B.C.)